The Complete Book of
Community Gardening

The Complete Book of Community Gardening

by Jamie Jobb

A Morrow Quill Paperback

William Morrow and Company, Inc.

New York / 1979

FIRST MORROW QUILL PAPERBACK EDITION

The Complete Book of Community Gardening was edited
and prepared for publication at the Yolla Bolly Press, Covelo,
California, during the spring and fall of 1978 under the
supervision of James and Carolyn Robertson. Production
staff: Sheila Singleton, Jay Stewart, Diana Fairbanks, Joyca
Cunnan, Gene Floyd, Barbara Speegle, Dan Hibshman, and
James Koss.

Grateful acknowledgment is made to the authors and pub-
lishers listed below for granting us permission to reprint
material originally published elsewhere.

The City People's Book of Raising Food. Copyright © 1975
by Helga and William Olkowski. Permission granted by
Rodale Press, Inc., Emmaus, Pa. 18049.

Eating in Eden. Copyright © 1976 by Ruth Adams. Permission granted by Rodale Press, Inc., Emmaus, Pa. 18049.

Food First. Copyright © 1977 by Frances Moore Lappe and
Joseph Collins. Permission granted by Houghton Mifflin
Company, Boston, Mass. 02107.

Worldwatch Paper 14 (October 1977) © Worldwatch Institute, 1977.

Library of Congress Cataloging in Publication Data

Jobb, Jamie.
  The complete book of community gardening.

  1. Community gardens. I. Title.
SB457.3.J62   635   78-23840
ISBN 0-688-03409-8
ISBN 0-688-08409-5 pbk.

Printed in the United States of America.

First Edition
1 2 3 4 5 6 7 8 9 10

THIS BOOK IS DEDICATED to Marion Bowen
and the wisdom and spirit of her true words.
"You can't solve all the world's problems at once,"
she said. "You've got to carry it in buckets.
A little bit at a time."

Contents

Part 3: Places   67

Part 4: Plants   101

Part 5: Possibilities   143

Part 6: Sources and Resources   163

Thanks

THIS BOOK IS the concerted result of a nationwide effort. These pages were abetted by and filled with the inspiring presence of:

Gilbert Wenger of Mesa Verde and Steve de Leon of La Junta, Colorado; Susan Charles of Louisville, Kentucky; Ben Davis of Atlanta; Mary and Art Crummer of Alachua, Florida; Jerry Pfeiffer and John Jobb of Gainesville, Florida; my parents of Miami.

Terry Porter and family of Indianapolis, Indiana; Ken Nicholls and Susan York Drake of Ann Arbor, Michigan; Peter Wotoweic of Cleveland; Clayton Knepley of Columbus, Ohio; Phyllis Mullen and Roger Dillard of Pomeroy, Ohio; William and Dorothy Morris, their children, and grandchildren centered in Middleport, Ohio.

Gil Friend and G. R. Shipman of Washington, D.C.; Linda Cohen of New York City; Ken Webb of Plymouth, Vermont. Stuart Leiderman on route somewhere to and from Drury, Missouri.

John and Deanne Lindstrom of Everett, Washington; Frances and Paul Jackson, Bruce Schwartz, Helen Weinstein of Los Angeles. Peter Brand, Rosemary Menninger, John Forbes, Susan O'Neill, Roy Swanson, Karen Paulsell, Joseph Torchia, and Robert Paul Builder of San Francisco. Also in California, Robert Kourik of Lagunitas, Nancy Beaubaire of Fairfax, Sue Stevens of Los Gatos, A.D. Adins and Lee Tecklenburg of Sacramento, John Dotter and Howie Simon of San Jose, Keith Muscutt and Richard Wilson of Santa Cruz, Tom Bassett and Richard Lee of Berkeley, Douglas McCoy and Wayne Cross of San Rafael, Raymond Chavez of Covelo.

Special assistance with research, language, networks, and preparation of the manuscript by Lynn Ferar, Diane Laufer, and Marilyn Wylder. Guidance by William C. Spann.

Introduction

THERE IS VERY LITTLE that is really rigorous or exacting about the natural aspects of gardening. Books and magazines can make it seem like such a difficult and complicated production. Indeed, this is an attitude most people have about a garden: it should be productive, efficient. It should operate like a machine, a business. It should be predictable, accountable, and held together by statistics.

But unless you're desperately trying to feed lots of people, gardening is no big academic deal that only experts or "green thumbs" can fully accomplish. Almost anything works in a garden — because gardens are moved by higher powers than human intelligence and foresight. Anything that doesn't grow will be replaced, if not by other human needs, then by nature's weeds. Gardening can be an act as basic as breathing, if the gardener is willing to fit unselfishly within the limits imposed by the unique nature of the place where the garden is situated.

For centuries, people everywhere have been gardening and farming, long before anyone knew how to write books about these things. Long before history dawned, people were putting seeds into the ground and taking advantage of what came out. Plants hold within their seeds and roots all their own secrets. All they require is their own time and room to grow. The gardener's responsibilities lie mostly in selecting the right plants to grow at the right time in the right spots, based on local conditions and varieties of plants that have adapted to these conditions.

Mark Malony of Contra Costa County Cooperative Extension puts it very well: "A lot of material you find in garden books and from the Cooperative Extension service is perhaps not really specific to your particular locale. It's very important that you take into consideration micro-climates and the regional nature of gardening."

Who knows the specifics of these local conditions best? People who have been gardening in the area for the longest time, the master gardeners in your neighborhood. They are the people who can best inform new gardeners about the particular local growing season, proper planting dates, and the most suitable varieties of common plants. These gardeners are one of the most valuable resources in any community, although they may be seldom recognized as such. They are not difficult to find, because their gardens stand out. The more of these gardeners you can find, the better off your group's garden will be.

Local nursery people, cooperative extension agents, colleges and other institutions may be able to help you. Asking them doesn't take much effort. By seeking advice from as many people as possible, you can begin to separate local fables from facts.

1
PURPOSE

Unsoiled Fingernails

SOME PEOPLE don't like to get their hands dirty, and *soil* is a dirty word to many home-makers. Subliminal hyperhygienic lessons are sponsored on TV and in other media. Prejudices against dirt, bugs, and the toils of "unskilled" labor lead to attitudes of biological overkill. The results of such unhealthy attitudes have surfaced most dramatically on the spotless supermarket shelves. The high cost of food is determined by advertising, packaging, and many other processes — things you can't eat.

Food prices begin with the high cost of land. Department of Agriculture statistics covering the bicentennial year indicate that the assessed value of farmland grew three times faster than the value of the crops and livestock produced upon it did. The land value of the average farm that year was $180,300, with the average acre costing over $450. The total value of U.S. agriculture real estate was almost $500 million.

Food prices are also affected by the costs of expensive modern equipment like disc harrows (opposite, bottom). Usually, the equipment needs to be financed, which adds to the expense. Also, a disc harrow cannot be used by itself. It needs something to pull it.

Modern tractors come in new models, just like Cadillacs. Added to the expense of the tractor and the financing of that expense are the shipping, parts, maintenance, gas, and oil — all of which are becoming more costly. Tractors create other economic ripples. In Guatemala, one tractor displaces four farmworkers. This was the home of many of the original farmers in the Western Hemisphere. They worked the soil centuries ago without machines.

Food, as we know it, requires transportation and storage. The farther it travels and the longer it is stored, the more expensive it becomes. Most of the grain raised, shipped, and stored in the U.S. — 78 percent — goes into animals, not people.

Guests at the Kansas City Stockyard are accommodated without luxury. But the costs here are hidden. For livestock to produce one pound of protein in the form of meat, an animal must consume 21.4 pounds of protein in the form of plants. The process is not efficient, especially when you consider that these animals are better fed than many people on this planet.

You can't eat the paper pushed across flavorless desks

and stuffed inside inedible filing cabinets, stacked inside tall, unpalatable buildings. Add to this the cost of office supplies and salaries of the people who don't handle a hoe at work.

Trucks, more gas, more oil, and space-age equipment all add to the rising costs of food. All machines need people to run and maintain them. These people need to be paid, and that adds again to the high price of food.

What This Book Is For

THIS BOOK IS FOR those of you who see squandered plenty all around, especially in the midst of large cities but elsewhere, too, in the most unlikely places. Lots of vacant land that no one cares for. Plenty of idle people with no land to call their own. Lots of untapped resources and unclaimed goods being wasted in official filing cabinets, dump sites, and soiled waters everywhere. Plenty of lots, scattered and left undone.

Not all such wealth is being squandered. Some people are learning to appreciate its value. In recent years, sundry groups of folks have staked out claims on vacant lots in their particular neighborhoods. There, on common ground and with common intentions, they have joined together to initiate gardens — gardens that emerge from human, as well as physical and metaphysical, potentials.

Usually these gardens are known as "community gardens" or sometimes "neighborhood gardens." People act as though these gardens are recent innovations, but they have evolved from ancient antecedents. In other places and other times, they have been called liberty gardens, victory gardens, leisure gardens, garden colonies, allotments, or simply nothing at all.

Labels are not as important as each garden's reason for being planted there. These reasons extend well beyond the borders of the garden.

FOOD FAST

A startling statistic was reported by the *New York Daily News* in its coverage of a recent summer meeting of four national food service organizations in that city. According to predications aired at the meeting, half of all meals eaten in the United States will be prepared and eaten away from home in the early 1980s. The report did not say how often gardeners were expected to be found eating away from home.

Most vacant-lot gardeners demand the right to safe and fresh food. Many are troubled by supermarket stabilizers, emulsifiers, preservatives, artificial flavorings, and other nonfood additives of dubious nutritional value. Some of these people even garden with the intentions of assuming the primary responsibility for their family's nutrition and health. It does not deter them to know that very few modern people have achieved dietary self-sufficiency. Many gardeners, feeling trapped in caged cities, also want to improve their surroundings and create blooming open space.

It is not always easy. Pollution and politics block the way in many places. But persistence in a few neighborhoods has established gardens permanent enough to support wells and windmills. Here gardeners won't be evicted; open space won't be erased.

Other community gardeners need noncompetitive but challenging forms of recreation. Many of them want to know more sides of a person than simply one — a fellow worker or tennis buddy or card partner. Instead, they want to know each other more completely. They envision the garden as a place for common understanding. Sometimes it is.

A few people seek to experience the mystic and seasonal rituals of nature and to be humbled under the unsolved mystery of them. With varying individual gardeners, other reasons will spring up. But ultimately, the group's intentions must be centered on the garden and its continued growth.

Single garden sites can include two families or more than a thousand, on lots as small as a single-family residence or an acreage as large as a farm. The operation of these gardens has assumed a multiplicity of forms. However, most gardens fit under one of two broad categories:

Informal: Usually small and located within walking distance of most gardeners' homes. Usually operate by word-of-mouth, as well as tightly organized plans, at least in the beginning. Sometimes aided but not run by civic clubs, institutions, and agencies.

Formal: Usually administered by an agency of city, county, or state government but not always. Concentrate large numbers of gardeners on single sites. Usually involve applications, fees, and less individual control over the garden's destiny, including important decisions about soil preparation, weeds, and pest management.

HEALTH AND TAX RELIEF

At that same conference, the *New York Daily News* also noted the words of Josephine Martin, president of the American School Food Service Association. "Six of ten killer diseases are food related. And fifty-two billion dollars is spent each year in hospitals in this country. When legislators and taxpayers realize the cost of poor nutrition, perhaps they will be more willing to put more money into the preventative measures."

SENSELESS DEFENSES

The Worldwatch Institute is a nonpolitical, nonprofit research organization that scrutinizes global problems and anticipates social trends. In a Worldwatch study titled *Redefining National Security,* the organization makes a very bold argument against further unchallenged tax expenditures alloted to the military defense of any country. Most countries on earth, according to the report, are in grave danger of having damn little worth defending.

"In fishery after fishery, the catch now exceeds the long-term sustainable yield," writes Lester R. Brown in the report. "The cutting of trees exceeds the regenerative capacity of forests almost everywhere. Grasslands are deteriorating on every continent as livestock populations increase along with human population. Croplands too are being damaged by erosion as population pressures mount. Failure to arrest this deterioration of biological systems threatens not only the security of individual nations but the survival of civilization as we know it."

COMMON UNITY GARDENS

"Could I have your attention please!"

Ready to talk but unsure of himself, he says his name is simply Jomo. This bright and bashful young man seems no older than twenty. He is a member of the Humboldt County Community Collective, attending a meeting of community garden organizers in California. All day people have been talking about their projects and problems. Jomo's garden project involves the elderly. All day he has waited for this chance.

"I've been kinda holding off from saying this, but I really feel it's important." He digs for the right words. "I'm sure that everybody knows from reading the papers and all that the world is going through a really very . . . heavy . . . time right now . . . ."

He hesitates. Maybe he should have picked another word? People want him to get to the point. An urgent fire starts to crack at the back of his voice.

"So it's really important . . . . What we're doing, by being involved in urban agriculture, is we're helping to heal the planet. And we're helping to hold things together. We're helping to hold people together . . . through these hard times right to look beyond the fact of our individual gardens and realize that what we're doing is, we're helping one another to get to know one another. . . . It goes far beyond the fact that we're raising radishes and raising carrots. It's helping us to realize our unity."

Primarily this book addresses itself to those running the first type of garden, but it includes much information of value to any garden project. Most community garden projects in the United States are of the formal kind. Many of them will help people in their regions who want to start other projects too. Some people realize that larger gardens involve energy expenditures — for travel and plowing — that would be better conserved by keeping the groups small, neighborly, and closer to home.

In gardens of any size, people need to recognize and use the existing wealth of resources that hide not only within each community but also within each individual.

These pages include more territory than is normally considered within the bounds of gardening. The book is concerned with cultural matters involving many interconnected communities of life. As we shall see, each successful garden must develop sentient tendrils that reach out into communities for acceptance and support.

These pages will begin with *people*. Time and again, neighborhood garden organizers have learned that the best way to begin their effort is with other interested people, not with vacant land. Bringing order to the land is often simple compared with the complex processes involved in bringing order to people.

After people, we will go on to *places*. For only after the group understands its purpose and organizes itself into a form that makes sense to all individuals involved, does the appropriate time arrive for serious searches into the best garden sites. Plenty of vacant land will probably be available, but looking at these lots selectively involves special considerations.

Next we will consider *plants* and related matters. All common garden plants fit within the greater supporting framework of plant families. Knowing these relationships leads gardeners to a fuller understanding of the myriad choices available before planting. Working with limited growing space, each community gardener must develop criteria for choosing when and where to plant what. Some gardens will require compost systems for improving sad soils. Gardeners will also need to understand more fully the proper place of bees, bugs, water, weather, and other natural forces within the whole experience of the garden.

Finally, we will consider . . . *possibilities*. As gardeners mature through each growing season, they will need to maintain contact and interest during the off seasons.

Organizers may get to know other nearby garden groups and exchange ideas with them. Adventuresome groups may wish to consider roof gardens, greenhouses, community canneries, land trusts, and other expansions of their efforts.

For humans, the next step of evolution may necessarily involve entire groups of people at once elevating themselves and others around them by changing perspectives, by paying more attention to nature and less to human happenstance. One way toward this evolutionary leap might be found through the very gates of opportunity opened by community gardens.

No one needs to own land in order to belong to one of these gardens. No one needs to be an experienced gardener — or a wealthy politician, although it certainly helps to know a few you can trust.

Long before historic time and all across the planet, groups of people have gotten together to grow gardens full of food. These plantings happen almost anywhere: near forests and grasslands, in pueblos at the edge of the desert, in prison on the edge of despair. In all cases, the gardens that thrive are the ones with gardeners who respect the special regional and local nature of their efforts.

We are members of the human community and are therefore bound to help or harm it by our behavior.

Wendell Berry

2
PEOPLE

Help Yourself

IT DOESN'T really matter what side of the continent you're on, Seattle or Miami, Boston or Sacramento. People everywhere are normally known and recognized first by their occupations. She's a lawyer or a poet. He's an adman or a dentist. But in a garden, someone may be known best for the beets she keeps or the cabbages he gives away. People have many sides, aspects, facets, interests, attitudes. Together, they combine and shine most brightly in a garden.

The military helped Clayton Knepley learn to be quick and observant. Clayton is retired but active. He teaches organic gardening classes and volunteers as a Cooperative Extension onsite assistant at Olentangy River Road Garden. He helps people with their problems and knows just about everything going on in the garden.

For example, here he points out an uncommon balsam pear plant grown by an Ohio State graduate student, who is interested in lesser known food plants. Knepley knows gardening can be exotic, but he also knows it is not difficult. You don't really need a lot of books and instruction about it. Knepley comes to this conclusion after reading a lot of books and attending a lot of classes.

Knepley knows community gardens aren't new either. When a fellow Columbus gardener said, "This is a European custom," Knepley was quick to correct him, "This is an American custom too!"

Days before this photo was taken, Thomas Young had been confined to a hospital in Harrisburg, Pennsylvania. For two weeks he was in intensive care, battling pneumonia.

Now, he spends much of his time in his garden plot at the Dauphin County Park and Recreation Garden Project, not far from the Pensylvania State capitol.

Thomas and his wife Maggie come from farming families. Searching for squashes is a natural pastime. Maggie would like to garden year around, but the Harrisburg garden program winds up in October.

Young is a very generous man. He gives you carrots, cucumbers; and he would probably share watermelon, corn, and beans if they were ready. You're not even recuperating! He hands you the squash he's holding here. "Help yourself," he says. "Sure. Help yourself."

Secrets from another world are hidden in the hearts and hands of this couple setting out stakes in the River Oaks Garden in Sacramento, California. Blacks, Filipinos, Mexican-Americans, as well as Orientals, garden together here.

You ask the couple about their garden methods, but they shrug. They can't talk to you; they don't know English. Besides they're too busy, and their garden plot speaks for itself.

Red leaf amaranth, bok choy, luffa, bitter melon, wax gourds, year-long beans, and strange celeries grow intensively here. Someone who speaks English says the couple spends most of each day here, just like many other people in this truly international garden.

Max Ross, a spry retired man of seventy, isn't particularly fond of weeds, but he knows which ones are edible. He leads you around his Indianapolis plot, pointing out lamb's quarters, purslane, broad-leafed plantain. Ross also has his eyes on a big stand of wild ground cherries that grow thick in a nearby forest. "They make the best jam you ever had," he says.

Ross and his wife Kathryn lease a big 50- by 50-foot lot from the Park and Recreation Department for fifteen dollars a year. This large allotment garden is located on the grounds of a former county poorhouse. Max and Kathryn have been gardening all their lives.

Poachers are a problem in this garden sometimes, but Max has learned to hide his melons under mulch and to keep a sharp eye out for strangers. There's still plenty of food to can, freeze, or otherwise stock up for winter. Although it was August, their freezer and pantry were almost full of corn, beans, tomatoes, squash; and they were getting ready to give the rest of the harvest away.

When this tree sprouted in the middle of Boston, Frances Kingman wasn't sure whether it was a peach or a papaya. Four years ago, she had tossed peach pits and papaya seeds into this corner of her plot in Fenway Garden. Now the tree has begun to show its fruit and let her know its name.

Peach trees are a luxury that are not available to many community gardeners. But Fenway is an unusual garden. Members in the Fenway Garden Society can keep a plot as long as they maintain it. Frances has had her spot here for twenty years. It's a happy jumble of fruits, berries, vegetables, herbs, and flowers that demonstrate her very special feeling for plants.

Although she is over sixty, she seems young and determined to deal with urban garden problems, including air pollution and stupid vandals who have ruined her peonies and coleus plants as well as vegetables. Fenway is unfenced. Hundreds of people pass through daily. But she has no intention of relinquishing her plot. "I don't have time to do all the things I want to do here," she says with regret.

Keeping plants watered and hoses neatly wrapped are two of Phil Chambers's many duties as a student assistant in the garden program at Cleveland's R.G. Jones School. Phil, seventeen at the time of this picture, helps students learn all aspects of gardening, including how to use the cold frames pictured below, which are presently not in use.

R.G. Jones is only one of fourteen tract gardens in the Cleveland school program, which has been in operation since 1904. Over twenty thousand students are involved annually in the program.

Phil explains that parents wanted a garden so badly they went to the school board and created a big fuss. It took a while, but they got the garden they demanded.

Phil likes his job because he gets to know "all the kids in the neighborhood." He wants to major in electronics at college, but he's worried he might get too interested in horticulture. "It just kinda grows on you," he smiles. "No pun meant there."

Origins of Gardening

BEFORE THIS CENTURY, food always grew very near to the place it was eaten and digested. Much of it was consumed uncooked. What people didn't eat right away was dried and stored for winter. No one had ever heard of refrigerators, preservatives, or interstate highways. Nonsense claims like "fresh" and "nutritious" were not printed on the natural "packages" that all food came in. Often the "packages" contained seeds as well as food. It took a while for people to figure seeds out, but eventually everyone understood what to do with those valuable specks of life. You saved them for the future.

Until modern times, food crops were usually eaten by the very people who grew them — groups of people. Usually they were all members of the same family or clan. But not always. They worked together, following family, community, or spiritual leaders who helped to determine when, where, and what to plant. Seeds and secrets stayed within families or were traded as precious commodities of exchange. Everyone expected birds, bugs, animals, and slippery people to steal, poach, or otherwise vandalize some of the crops. Everyone lived with nature's nasty inconveniences by planting more than needed. Many enjoyed the experience, although some considered it "work." At least everyone had enough to eat, most of the time. When hunger spread, it was caused by natural disasters more than by man-made ones.

In less than one hundred years, machines have rearranged people's priorities. Only in the last three decades have people known the dubious luxury of bright electric supermarkets and frozen fast foods. Automobiles have allowed families and clans to divide and conquer themselves with hundreds of highway miles. People have become less bound to work on community projects together, without question and without pay. Few assume any of the vital responsibilities for feeding themselves. New kinds of fancy farm and restaurant machines do most of the work anyway. Diets change in subtle but drastic ways.

The Ambiguous Community

The origins of community gardens can be traced well beyond the shoreline of recorded time, back to the very beginnings of communities and gardens themselves. In fact, the farther back you go, the more meaningless words like *garden* and *community* become.

Prehistoric farms were probably more like some places now considered gardens. They were small, nearby, diverse, manageable, and distinctly human. They were economically organized but scaled to family and animal dimensions. When these "farms" got too big and too monotonous, problems with erosion, water, and pests ensued. This has happened before in other places. It is happening now, and it will probably happen again.

What is a community anyway? Throughout most of history, family clans clearly defined everyone's place in society. People knew where they fit into the system and what they could expect in return.

But in modern urban times, you can belong to several communities at once: family, friends, neighborhood, fellow employees, people who happen to have the same color of skin. The modern community is a relative concept, but it has little to do with blood relations. Modern communities are unrelated folks who join together as a matter of necessity or desire. People apparently like to belong to groups, no matter what miracles they accomplish or squander together.

Roots for the word *community* reach back to the Latin word *communis* which meant "common," as in commonplace and common ground and common sense. According to the dictionary, a community can be any group of people living in the same place with the same government, same social class, same society, same possessions, same activities, same interests. Community can also

"Cities as we know them grew as
both workers and owners, through
industrialization, sought the riches
of life." Thus Frank Smith of the
Public Resources Center describes
the rise of urban attractions and
distractions. In cities, "food, like
other essentials, is produced by
strangers at great distances and is
available in supermarkets only
for money."

mean the very place itself. And the place could be as big as the community's reasons for being together. For example, members of the Mexican-American community reside in several states.

A community, then, would be any group of people with something in common. The more complexities in people's lives, the more communities they may belong to and, ironically, the less they might find entirely in common.

Today the phrase *community garden* has come to mean almost any group of people with one place in common — a garden. Here they raise food, relax, create, recreate, learn about life, share handy ideas, swap squashes and tomatoes. Most of the gardens are arranged with individual plots for families or single people. Some gardens have common plots where everyone can share in the preparing, planting, selection, cultivation, growth, harvest, and enjoyment of the plot. In the late 1970s, community gardens could be found in every state, especially those with large urban areas.

"As urbanization has increased,
the American diet has deterio-
rated, so that it is now seriously
deficient with regard to certain
nutrients and is detrimental in
its high caloric content, low
ratio of polyunsaturated to sat-
urated fatty acids and lack of
fiber, these being diet characteristics which are thought to
contribute to hypertension,
heart disease, and cancer of the
colon. An increase in fruit and
vegetable intake by the American populace would alter these
diet characteristics in a positive
way and therefore has the potential for reducing levels of
these degenerative diseases and
would reduce deficiencies of
vitamin A, vitamin C, and iron
in the population."

Jean W. Smith, Associate Professor of Interdisciplinary Sciences at the University of the
District of Columbia, aired
these remarks at a panel of the
Urban Food Conference held
in Washington, D.C., during
the bicentennial.

Feeling Rootless

Without roots in land or family, many modern folks feel estranged from basic human rites, unsettled, rootless, restless. People removed from relatives and seasonal fluctuations are not humbled by nature.

Modern writers, Wendell Berry foremost among them, speak of the "necessity of wildness" or "rituals of return to the human condition." Others talk simply in terms of getting "back to land." It's generally acknowledged that people need lots more than a secure roof, clean clothes, and three squares a day. Something of spirit and of substance is .missing. Evidence of this is found in traffic jams of campers filing out of the cities on Friday to soak up scenery before returning again in a jam on Sunday. Obviously cooped beyond tolerable limits, city people need to flee their modern bewilderness and search for the divine links with nature hiding inside themselves and the others around them.

The same natural, seasonal laws that make themselves felt in a rural setting likewise exert themselves in a garden. But gardens urge natural mysteries to occur closer to home.

Therapeutic Nature

Academicians have begun to recognize the uplifting physical, mental, and spiritual aspects of gardens, especially gardens growing with more than one gardener. In some states — including Delaware, Florida, Georgia, Kansas, Michigan, Rhode Island, South Carolina, and Texas — colleges have instituted degree programs in "horticultural therapy." In these programs, students learn to recognize and design gardens as sanctuaries from the vague irregularities of concrete urban life.

Nutritional Truths

Gardens most always share one common aspect: They exist primarily to feed people. Individual plots in community gardens are predominated by vegetables and fruits. Nutrition, health, and pleasurable eating are obvious concerns as vacant-lot gardeners seek more control over the variability and stability of their diets.

Diane and J. Randall Wheaton share a 20- by 40-foot plot with another couple at Ann Arbor's Ecology Center Garden on the University of Michigan's north campus. Diane is outspoken about their purpose there. "The main reason we joined the garden was so we could grow food without a lot of chemicals in it," she says. "My husband is a chemist, and he's very concerned about chemicals in the food supply. It even bothers us to be gardening near the road, where there's so much lead from the cars. Although, we figure it's probably better than most of the food we get in the stores."

Joined in gardens together, neighbors are seeking old as well as new solutions to common food problems. Some fly the banner of "urban agriculture" and assume tasks well outside the usual realms of gardening, animal husbandry for instance. Some city folks raise goats, chickens, rabbits, ducks, and fish for food and fertilizer production. At a unique place in San Francisco known simply as "The Farm," poultry and other animals live next to a freeway in a large warehouse room with straw spread on the floor and a false forest of still-green conifers cut and rammed into place between the floor and ceiling. The straw and pine scents mix with animal aromas to give the room a rural air that's rarely encountered in an urban setting.

OVERFED AND UNDERDEVELOPED

"Within a few years from the time Eskimos, American Indians, or Africans leave their ancestral home and diets and move to town where they eat 'civilized' diets, they rapidly fall prey to 'the diseases of civilization.' "

The author is Ruth Adams, the first managing editor of *Prevention* magazine. The quotation appears in her book *Eating in Eden: The Nutritional Superiority of Primitive Foods.* She continues, "What are these diseases? Obesity and overweight, diabetes, coronary heart conditions involving strokes and heart attacks, circulatory troubles including varicose veins, hemorrhoids, and hardening of the arteries, peptic ulcers, tooth decay, diverticulitis, colitis, constipation, hiatal hernia, gallstones, varicocele, and possibly many more conditions which are common in 'civilized' countries."

What are the main nutritional causes at the root of these diseases? Ruth Adams cites too much white sugar and refined starches, along with a distinct lack of fresh greens, vegetables, and fruits in most "civilized" diets.

In Ann Arbor, Diane Wheaton points to adzuki beans she planted as an experiment. She just planted beans that she had bought in a health food store. The beans are thriving. Elsewhere community gardeners experiment with other uncommon garden foods like chayote, amaranth, winged beans, bitter melons, balsam pears, taro, and other plants with lesser known names — plants whose nutritional and culinary values have not yet been completely realized. These experimenters find community gardens a great place to learn about uncommon plants along with their neighbor gardeners — especially those who have maintained strong ties to their homelands of Mexico, Peru, China, Japan, Puerto Rico, Cuba, Polynesia, and other places where family contact with soil and seed may still be strong and unbroken for centuries.

Dependently Healthy

Mark Casady grew up in a family with a broad background in civic and agricultural affairs. Among his relatives, he finds a newspaper publisher, a banker, a judge and founding father of Des Moines, as well as partners in a hybrid seed corn company. This background has shaped his view of himself and his purpose in life. At times he has tended livestock, sold fertilizer, organized a commune, worked in orchards, fields, construction, and

GARDEN FORMS

Any group's garden can assume many forms, depending on the group and what it believes to be its purposes.

Neighborhood vacant lot: Nearby and usually small. Composed of family, friends, and neighborly people. Similar to victory garden concept, but also based on new attitudes toward energy and nutrition. People usually walk to these gardens.

Community allotments: Large gardens with scores, even hundreds, of plots in one place. Usually administered by a local civic agency. Most of the work to establish the garden — site selection, clearing and preparing soil — is done for you. Usually a fee and transportation access are involved.

Apartments: Most logical place for many urban gardens is a housing project, as people in Chicago, New York, Sacramento, and other cities have learned. Apartment houses with no room for a garden on their own grounds can use nearby vacant land.

Common farms: Usually a collective with common fields, not plots. Sometimes found in more rural settings. Gardeners barter, give away, or share produce.

Park and recreational: More permanent because they are established on parkland. Room may be provided at garden site for playgrounds, picnic areas; open spaces for games and other recreation.

Employee allotments: Established by an employer. Part of the business property is reserved for gar-

dening. A place to relax during breaks, lunch, or rush hour.

School or youth: Often, but not always, administered by the school system. Kids and sometimes parents garden on school grounds under supervision and a precisely scheduled sequence. Gardens may be part of environmental education programs.

Institutional: Gardens on grounds of institutions for elderly, disabled, juveniles, and others who realize the therapeutic values of horticulture. Food from these gardens nourishes people in the dining hall as well.

Demonstration-Research: Place to educate the public, as well as try new ways of gardening. Sometimes involves selection and breeding of new varieties of plants.

newspapers. Now he is the energetic director of Los Angeles Neighborhood Gardens and Farms. Mark does not see these gardens serving primarily as recreation or therapy. His main concern is for what community gardens can add to someone's plate.

"A lot of people are starving and just dying in our culture, and we don't even realize it," Casady says. "Lots of these people are eating too much sugar, drinking too much booze, and smoking too many cigarettes. And they are not getting enough good food . . . . A lot of them are poor people. They need help, the kind of strength people can get from a garden. I want to go right to these neighborhoods because that's where the human ecology problem is and that's where the gardens belong."

Any Means Necessary

Able neighbors join together to start gardens for many reasons besides the common ones: improving diets and nutritional wisdom, offering therapy outdoors, expanding leisure and recreational options, supplanting rootlessness, resurrecting rituals, and fulfilling open space.

People also garden together for companionship and friendship, for involvement in neighborhood and community improvement and restoration, for family pleasure

Some folks call their efforts, "urban agriculture" and they mean it. One place you'll find true urban farmers — people who raise animals as well as plants — is Berkeley, California. The goat pictured here resides at the University of California Urban Food Garden, just a quick walk from the campus and downtown. Several rabbits are also housed here. Besides providing a source of food, these animals eat excess green matter and act as walking compost piles. The Organic Farmers of Berkeley plan to raise ducks and chickens, as well as goats and rabbits, at their new farm in the industrial section of town.

and social pastime, to watch things grow or to get lost in thought, to become more self-reliant and to improve the topsoil for others who follow. Some people picture gardens eventually evolving into neighborhood centers where youngsters learn about nature while grownups swap seeds and stories about the better world they are seeking.

Each neighborhood can add its own reasons for starting a garden to this list. But eventually neighbors must find the means to rally reasons into realities before a garden can sprout and stretch to the sun. Necessity should dictate the path any group takes, doing it neighborly and informally or enlisting the formal aid of civic agencies and community groups. Perhaps a bit of both would work. No matter what form the garden takes, be advised that there are always ways to accomplish it.

Closer to Home

COMMUNITY-MINDED GARDENS sprout out of a self-appointed "seed bunch." Others may call this a "steering committee," "pilot council," "core group," or any other name that means virtually the same thing. Depending on the scope and size of the project, this seed group may consist of as few as two people or well over a dozen. Their initial agenda is to determine: interest in the project, location and form of the garden, requirements for membership, and primary methods for handling major tasks such as preparing soil or arbitrating squabbles. The seed bunch can also expect to do little things like staking out individual plots or cooking up compost heaps, until these become the established responsibilities of a concerned cluster of gardeners at the site.

People in the seed bunch make decisions and get things done, at least until the garden grows enough to be influenced by natural forces within it and outside forces from the surrounding communities. Seed people are dedicated to researching choices, gathering resources, setting schedules, and assuring that tasks will be seen through to completion. Often this includes doing much of the work themselves. But they probably don't consider it real work. All their efforts are aimed at growing themselves a garden closer to home. And that's not really work. It's a pleasure.

Family, Friends, Acquaintances

Any seed bunch is composed primarily of friends, acquaintances, and maybe a few family members. Usually they're all people willing to get to know one another better.

Decisions and maneuvers in seed group meetings may not always be rational, predictable, or democratic. Someone may suddenly drop out. The group will falter and sometimes grow despite itself. Soon it will become clear that no single individual can honestly take credit for the group's propitious (or sometimes preposterous) decisions to act the way it does.

As the garden grows, the seed bunch will diminish in importance. This diminishing may occur in direct proportion to the effectiveness of the systems that seed people establish and the emergence of an experienced core of gardeners, who know how to take care of group responsibilities themselves.

Goals and Boundaries

The first order of business for the seed bunch should be a natural one. Everyone must take the necessary time and patience required to get to know one another. All seed members need to state as clearly as they can their goals, purposes, intentions, and limitations about being together. Each one should understand what the others expect to give and get from the garden.

If you can afford to start a garden, ask yourself the following questions. It might help to put the answers down on paper.

How much time and energy are you willing to invest, so others in the group can rely on you? What's your attitude about continuing to volunteer your time to help the garden get started? Would you consider being paid to keep the garden growing?

What leisure, recreational, or other aspects of your present life must you relinquish in order to have time for the garden project? What is the largest number of people you can anticipate enjoying a garden with? Primarily what do you expect to reap from the experience of the garden besides food? Anything else?

Getting Along with Each Other

In working to establish the garden, everyone in the seed group will presumably have the same initial purpose. Everybody likely will be starting on the same wavelength. But it would be a hasty presumption to expect everyone to remain in laser-perfect focus.

Indeed, it's not easy to stay on beam. As the seed bunch grows during its initial meetings, people are prone to hang out their wills and won'ts. Sometimes someone's feelings get stepped on. This hurts and diverts energy.

Later the seed group is bound to have big disagreements about important matters ("Shall we charge a fee for each plot?"), as well as arguments about silly things ("What color should the gate be painted?"). After long-winded and wasted hours, someone will suddenly discover that everybody wasn't as opposed as they had originally seemed.

Sometimes it's best just to keep your mind shut to the specifics of battle and keep your mouth tuned to more productive channels. The fewer individuals willing to slip into futile fights, the shorter the fights will be. Most of you will need to forget that stuff you learned in school about being competitive anyway. This is the real world, where cooperation, graciousness, and finesse outscore opposition.

Window-Shopping for Land

Early in its life, members of the seed bunch no doubt will begin to keep a casual mental inventory of vacant lots in the neighborhood. Potential garden sites spring from obscurity once people begin paying closer attention to their surroundings.

Someone might learn what activities were located on a particular parcel before it became vacant. Seasoned gardeners may also note how the soil looks, smells, and feels. But knowledgeable vacant-lot gardeners realize that these first impressions can be deceiving. What seems to be a perfectly good site now, might not appear so perfect upon further study of the economic and ecologic factors.

It's okay to window-shop for sites, but no one should be serious about settling yet. You'll have lots of time to find good garden spots, but now the group needs to concentrate more on its own formation. Anyway, only after vital statistics are gathered on the neighborhood's potential interest, will the seed group have a solid basis for determining which sites are most centrally located and how much space is needed for plots, picnic areas, quiet spots, and common grounds dedicated to aromas and other luxuries of the garden.

FIRST THINGS FIRST

Here are some guidelines that each person should keep in mind during the first couple of seed group meetings.

Get to know each other's aspirations and reasons for being there.

Clearly establish the purposes and scope of the group. Put them into writing, if necessary.

Determine how much energy and time each person is willing to devote to the project.

Find out what each individual will give up from their current activities in order to assist the garden.

Establish the form of the garden.

Proceed slowly so the project is manageable.

Don't pick or join fights.

Maintain contact with each other between meetings to keep informed of new developments.

Tell stories that uplift spirits.

Anything else that comes to the group's mind.

As the seed group takes form
during the first few weeks, new
considerations will crop up.
These will vary greatly, according to the particulars of each
project. But any group should
expect to:

Define the boundaries of res-
idency for eligible gardeners.

Set a preliminary limit on the
number of people the garden
should accommodate.

Limit the number of garden sites
you are willing to establish in the
first season.

Draw up a tentative timetable.
Define the tasks that need to be
handled immediately and in the
near future.

Make a preliminary matching of
tasks and people. Make sure the
task suits each person's talents,
capabilities, and interests.

Give the group a name.

And so on.

Necessarily a Name

Eventually members of the seed group will begin to think about a name for the projected garden, a name that transmits an image of what the effort is all about. This is not only to communicate to the neighborhood and public at large but to the gardeners themselves. A name that neatly identifies the group for everyone and fits easily into your concepts and conversations about the garden is needed.

Names can be serious. *Mi Tierra* Garden, sponsored by San Jose California Park and Recreation and Food Bank programs, means "my land" in Spanish. Names can be light. One garden among the eight in Ann Arbor's Project Grow chose "Turn-up Green" as their handle.

Everyone should always allow room for people to change their minds about the project as they learn more about it. Those who remain rigid and steadfast in their outlook will only create chaos, trouble, and obstacles.

It will take a while to determine any seed group's unique reasons for being together. But this must be grappled with before moving on to more serious matters and especially before making any effort to reach out and contact others about joining the project.

To keep the project manageable, it's best to move slowly through this early formative period. The seed bunch should concentrate on one task at a time. Get it done and move on to the next. Seed members should often reassure themselves that each task fits current priorities.

On Being Neighborly

For the sake of energy conservation, nutrition, fresh-ness, and taste, it makes good common sense for food to be grown as close to home as possible. And not only in neighborhoods but anywhere — as locally as can be.

Exactly how big is your neighborhood? Have you ever stopped to measure it? The seed bunch will need to estab-lish a working definition of the neighborhood and its boundaries. This definition can be specifically amended or redefined later. For now, it will serve as a basic refer-ence for everyone during the time before the garden site is determined.

This information will also help set preliminary limits on the size of the garden. Each seed member by now should have set a rough limit on the number of people he or she would feel comfortable gardening with on one spot. For simplicity's sake, everyone can think in terms of five, ten, fifteen, twenty, twenty-five, or more gardeners. From there it's simple multiplication to determine the necessary size of the site. The number of anticipated gardeners times the complete square footage of one anticipated plot gives the total area needed for planting. Then the area for pathways and common spaces has to be estimated, to calculate the total area that will be needed.

Eventually the seed group will have to outline residence requirements, if it expects to stay small. It must also establish a timetable, if it expects to click into operation. Begin any schedule by establishing a preliminary listing of appropriate tasks and people who can handle them. These listings should be considered flexible, at least until the group's leadership is well established.

Leaders and Doers

Any seed bunch will talk about all kinds of ideas. But if the group wants to bring forth more than idle speculation, someone at some point must act on the best of those ideas. With luck everyone in the seed group will comprehend the distinction between talk and action.

Elected leaders are picked mostly through images of popularity. But first natural leaders select themselves, usually by their straightforward actions within the seed group. Most of these leaders work through directly visible effects. Other leaders work best through minds and words. They enjoy cultivating social graces as well as carrots. This kind belongs in the community, mustering support in the form of materials, land, money, or water.

Followers can be sheep or rams, depending not only upon their leaders but also on their feelings about themselves and their effectiveness within the group. Good followers don't simply take orders. They can reorient themselves for alternative solutions to new problems that surface after a leader leaves.

A good seed group leader must quickly learn to recognize subtle variations in interest among individuals and to act with genuine respect for these interests.

45

PROJECT LEADER

The person who leads the project must be primarily attuned to people and programs in the community. The project leader must also know gardening well enough to represent the gardeners' needs and wishes. For example, anytime you decide to expand beyond one site, the project leader would be the logical choice for coordinating the entire program. The project leader has these responsibilities:

Know the information resources of your area — libraries, city hall, colleges, the press, other institutions — and how to use them.

Know and respect the neighborhood power structure, so your group doesn't unwittingly step on anyone's toes.

Enlist the support of community groups, associations, and agencies.

Approach groups that can volunteer to assist the garden in some way.

Invite soil specialists, entomologists, plant breeders, horticulturists to tour the garden and discuss specific problems with interested gardeners.

Act as final arbiter of arguments, especially between gardeners and the garden's immediate neighbors.

RESOURCE PERSON

If your project proceeds for a time without a budget, you'll need a sharp, energetic person to round up materials and keep track of services and resources available in your area. A resource person must know how to scavenge as well as how to create new sources of materials. In addition this person should:

Determine the materials that the garden will need.

Create a system to handle future needs as they occur.

Survey the neighborhood to determine sources of scavengeable materials.

Survey your town to find which agencies and organizations can assist you.

Research garden literature for new systems, materials, technologies, and ideas.

Keep the bulletin board current and readable.

Reserve a bulletin board spot to list needed materials, resources, and services.

Keep an expandable listing of area materials and resources.

Be sure the listing is coherent so others can use it.

GARDEN PERSON

One person must take complete responsibility for coordinating the garden site. This person should be a knowledgeable gardener but must also be people oriented. Some folks call the person who does this task the site coordinator. You may prefer the term garden person. Under whatever name, these persons, by their actions and insights, usually determine whether the entire garden flourishes or fails. The garden person should:

Help gardeners determine what varieties of vegetables and fruits grow best in your area.

Work with inexperienced gardeners who want help in planning and preparing plots.

Provide direction in soil preparation.

Find the answers to gardeners' specific questions.

Enlist the aid of experienced gardeners.

Know how to identify plants, bugs, and other creatures for those who don't know.

Maintain information on water, compost, trash, tools, and other garden systems.

Plant a demonstration plot.

Deal with abandoned, weed-infested plots.

Tap Cooperative Extension and other horticultural agents for printed information and materials.

Arbitrate disagreements, especially those involving pesticides, herbicides, and other questionable products.

CONTACT PERSON

If the project attracts more than two dozen gardeners or more than one garden site, the group will need to establish a position for a contact person. This position should be more than the equivalent of a secretary. The contact person's primary responsibility is coordinating information between and among gardeners and the outside world. Specifically this should include these duties:

Keep minutes of meetings and other important notes filed so others can find them.

Coordinate media and neighborhood outreach efforts.

Be primarily responsible for mailings.

Handle phone messages. If there is no phone near the garden, the person's home phone may become the garden switchboard.

Help account for phone and mail costs if they become budget items.

Help lead tours and classes if the garden becomes a demonstration site.

Exchange information with those who need it.

Locate and coordinate volunteers. Know the particular delicacies of handling people who offer their spare time.

Electing People

Eventually, the simple tasks that move the project forward must be elevated to the level of assumed responsibilities. Everyone in the seed group must be alert to the right time for establishing and selecting precise positions of leadership.

Three preliminary positions need to be considered. These are the project leader, the garden person, and the resource person. If the seed group expects to grow beyond one site or twenty-five gardeners, add a fourth position, the contact person. If the group expects to chase and handle money, add a fifth position, the money person.

Naturally, because the project leader presides over the project, this person must be oriented primarily toward people and community involvement. However, to fully represent the gardeners' points of view, the project leader must also have a current and thorough understanding of the needs and problems of the garden.

The garden person's primary responsibility is orderly growth at the eventual site. This person must be an experienced gardener who can answer difficult questions and solve unique problems that pop up.

The resource person should actively catalog and tap services available within surrounding communities. This person should find out exactly which groups, organizations, agencies, and institutions can aid the garden in specific ways.

MONEY PERSON

Any group that expects to handle money will need someone to do more than just keep track of it. This money person not only needs to keep a budget and account for it, but he or she must also be versed in writing proposals and grant applications for future funding. In addition the money person should:

Determine what money is needed for what purposes (fences, land, security, water, pipe, tools, insurance, salaries).

Establish budget priorities and keep track of each item.

Work closely with the resource person to understand what can be found free, donated, or bought on sale.

Check into local, state, and federal sources of funds, in that order. These funds might be earmarked for open space, recreation, nutrition, or other areas that could be applied to community gardening.

Determine the needs and sources for future funding.

All Responsible for One

Elected garden leaders have the ultimate responsibility to see that necessary tasks are accomplished. But each individual gardener has responsibilities to everyone else in the group. These responsibilities will vary greatly among groups, but they will include simple as well as complex things. Examples might be double checking to see that the water is turned completely off and the gates are closed, or detecting pests and diseases in your plot that could affect neighbor plots. This could even mean destroying and removing plants from your plot so the problem doesn't spread around the garden.

Blooming Through Outreach

THE SEED GROUP has sprouted and laid ground rules for its efficient operation. Now it's time to gather the interest of the immediate neighborhood and the overall community in the very idea of a garden. What are the best ways to determine this interest?

When potential garden groups in Sacramento, California, contact Lee Tecklenburg, coordinator of that county's extensive garden program, he asks four questions: Is the group organized? How many families are interested? Does anyone have possible sites in mind for the garden? Has the group conducted an outreach?

Outreach means simply reaching out to the neighborhood to inform people about the project and invite anyone to join or otherwise assist the effort. The group can find all kinds of ways to conduct this outreach. Newspapers, radio, and TV exist, in part, on information coming from community groups and projects. The group can also print and distribute its own handbills, flyers, or newsletter. Or the effort can be strictly personal, door-to-door, word-of-mouth. A few groups plan parades, fairs, and workshops to attract continued interest in an established garden.

There are all kinds of ways for people to hear about your group, but there's only one way they'll respond to the outreach — if they're interested. Those who are will have more than enough reasons for joining the garden, so there's no need to be pushy.

The seed bunch should extend its first outreach effort to those in the neighborhood who may be interested in joining the projected garden. Later, the group may want to conduct another kind of outreach to find supporters, volunteers, donors, and others who can lend time, money, supplies, land, or any other assistance the garden needs.

In either case, the group's resource person or contact person should keep a current listing of all those who seriously respond to each outreach. One good way to do this is on three by five cards filed in a recipe box. Be sure the cards are clearly written and filed under categories that everyone can understand.

How Far Outreach?

Naturally, if the group anticipates a small garden, the initial outreach efforts should be kept small, especially those aimed at arousing potential gardeners. The group can keep matters local by using mail, handbills, personal outreach tactics.

If seed members are determined to find as many gardeners as possible, they will need help from a broad spectrum of the community. This requires an outreach extended through the media, where lots of potential gardeners and public assistance can be courted. This is also where those who help can be publicly thanked.

Each time the group begins an outreach effort, these questions should be answered as firmly as possible. Exactly what is the nature of the support being sought? Who and where is the audience that needs to be reached? What are the best ways and media to reach this audience? Exactly why is this the best time to take the matter before the public? How well prepared is the group to handle those who respond?

Talking Through Media

When the seed group feels an urge to reach an audience outside the neighborhood, the message may need to be sent through the media. This involves certain rules and courtesies.

No bona fide community group should have to demand or beg for media coverage. The purpose of the

An outreach effort can take many forms, depending on whom you're trying to reach. Many times during the life of the garden, you may need to speak directly to the people of the neighborhood. The simplest way to say what you want is in person and in print. Instant presses and copy machines make this easy. Then you just mail your information or nail it to a pole.

However, there are other times when you'll need to contact more people than you can attract with your own printing efforts. Various media in your area exist for this reason. The main element in any successful media outreach is good timing. Be sure to allow for bulk mail sluggishness.

Below are four types of outreach that are sometimes combined into one effort.

1. Personal outreach: door-to-door, phone networks, word-of-mouth, slide shows, neighborhood tours, trucks and other vehicles, local characters.

2. Mail and nail outreach: handbills, flyers, leaflets, posters, bulletins, newsletters, signs, magic letterheads, bulk mail permit.

3. Media outreach: press releases, public service announcements, press kits, "a press friend," news or features.

4. Public outreach: parades, fairs, festivals, cookouts, harvest parties, moonlight dances, workshops, and classes.

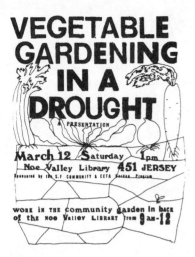

Some people put lots of effort into posters, handbills, flyers, and other bulletins announcing parades, fairs, and special events. For these to stand out on bulletin boards and walls, they should contain clear artwork and a key phrase in large lettering.

Bilingual handbills, flyers, posters, questionnaires, and even newsletters are necessary in some areas. Los Angeles County flyers must contain both Spanish and English. If you can't find a translator, check with local colleges or universities. People in the foreign language departments can probably find someone to help you.

press is to find out what groups like yours are doing. Keep this foremost in mind. However, the sad fact is that TV and radio are designed so that most newsworthy messages longer than a couple of minutes do not cross the airwaves. Newspapers have similar space limitations. Many groups have learned that the best way to send messages through the media is to keep them brief and to the point. This necessarily involves lots of editing before media releases are mailed.

Also beware of dumb games that members of the press sometimes play. Many newspeople are looking for a good fight, and some will go to great lengths to find one. As a result, well-meaning groups have been dragged into needless battles and made to look foolish or frivolous. Such a development can delay, confuse, or derail your group's effort. So take it easy. And take this advice from Cora Orr, a coordinator of the Richmond (California) Garden Project: "Get to know a press friend."

A Press Friend

No one outside the seed group will be more valuable to the formation of the garden than a good friend (or friends) among the news media. This is someone who not only sees the newsworthiness of your efforts, but also maintains genuine interest in the group beyond its immediate usefulness as a news source. This someone can help immeasurably with short cuts, advice, and contacts leading elsewhere within the community and the media.

Ideally, the project leader or contact person should cultivate this friendship. However, it helps to understand that press people are beings of the moment. Time is their bread and accuracy their butter. Be direct, tell stories straight, provide background information when necessary. That's the way to speak the press language.

Finding a press friend will take a while, unless you discover someone intuitively interested in the project, someone who sees a wealth of possibilities for "human interest" and other news blooming in the garden. Perhaps, you'll find someone who will eventually want to join you as a gardener!

The best way to begin looking is by studying newspapers and broadcasters to determine who has the apparent responsibility for covering efforts such as yours. Most

COOPERATIVE EXTENSION
UNIVERSITY OF CALIFORNIA

Community Agriculture and Nutrition Program
Room 200
1833 W. 8th Street
Los Angeles, CA 90057
(213) 736-2445

Common Ground
Tierra Comun

TO: Public Affairs Director
FOR RELEASE: Immediate
CONTACT: John Pusey
PHONE: 213 736-2577

GARDEN FAIR #4   20 seconds.

Here's good news for everyone who wants to become healthy, wealthy,
and wise.

There will be an entertaining and informative "GARDEN FAIR" on Saturday,
September 10th, from 11 AM to 4 PM, at the Columbia Community Garden,
4371 W. 190th St. in Torrance.

The fair will be open to all those interested in growing fresher, tastier
and more nutritious vegetables in their home or community garden.

Admission is free. So for a fun and informative afternoon, plan to attend.

TO: All Media
FOR RELEASE: Immediate
CONTACT: John Pusey
PHONE: 213 736-2577

EDUCATIONAL GARDEN FAIR PLANNED FOR SEPTEMBER 10TH IN TORRANCE

Here's good news for everyone who wants to become healthy, wealthy and wise!

The University of California Co-operative Extension, in conjunction with the
City of Torrance Department of Park and Recreation, will hold an entertaining
and informative "GARDEN FAIR" for all those interested in growing fresher,
tastier and more nutritious vegetables in their home or community gardens.

The Fair will be open to all, with no admission charge, from 11 AM until 4 PM,
on Saturday, September 10th. Location of the day's activities will be the
Columbia Community Garden, at 4371 W. 190th St. in Torrance.

The many topics to be explored by representatives of the University's
Community Agriculture and Nutrition Program include: the best vegetable
varieties for Los Angeles; intensive gardening (or how to get the most from
the least!); herbs; water conservation; the safe use of pesticides; and
nutrition tips with special recipes. There will also be demonstrations on
soil preparation, vegetable judging, weed identification, and tool maintenance. Youths from local 4-H groups will sponsor exhibits and be on hand to
answer questions on the care and feeding of animals.

The general public is invited. For a fun and informative day, including
refreshments, music, games and a drawing for prizes, plan to attend the
"GARDEN FAIR" September 10th.

---

*Public service announcements
should be timed exactly to fill
spots of various lengths — five,
ten, fifteen, twenty, thirty seconds or whatever the station requires. PSAs should be typed
double spaced on stationery that
carries the group's letterhead. Be
certain to include the name and
phone number of someone to
contact for further information.
A press release contains more
complete information than can
be shoehorned into short PSAs.
However, fill-in-the-blank press
releases look too much like form
letters and are usually less
effective.*

FREE AIR TIME

Free broadcast time is available to
garden groups through local radio
and TV stations. Each station's
license requires that free time be
given to community groups for
public service announcements —
or PSAs. In some cities, PSAs are
broadcast at odd hours, and this
limits their effectiveness. However,
most groups are content with the
free exposure, and besides, doing
PSAs helps the group become
known to broadcasters who may
want to learn more about the
group for future reference.

In order to reserve time for a PSA,
you must:

Pick stations with audiences you
intend to reach.

Talk about the garden project
with the public affairs director
or other person at the station who
is responsible for PSAs.

Determine the station's requirements, including length of announcements.

Write spot announcements to fit
within allotted time slots.

Complete other requirements (supply tape recordings, appear in person at the right time, whatever).

If anyone knows a willing film-
maker or video journalist, the
group may be able to produce its
own short PSAs for TV.

MEDIA RELEASE

Any news release from a seed
group should answer the journalist's five — sometimes six — basic
questions for telling news:
Who? What? When? Where? How?
And, sometimes, why? After those
facts are clear, the release can
move on to whatnot, or other information of human interest.

A press release should arrive at
its destination at least a week in
advance of the event foretold. If
the planned event is big (a parade,
fund raiser, or other large affair),
a series of media releases, each
timed to arrive at a specified date,
may be in order.

news writers have beats — or areas of expertise. Depending on the size and organization of local newspapers, the logical first choice is the garden editor. You might also try leisure, entertainment, features, family, or food editors. All of them could conceivably view neighborhood gardens as part of their beat. If you are unable to determine the names of these people, contact the city editor, or the person responsible for assigning reporters to cover local news.

Broadcasters generally do not have such a broad variety of special writers. If you can't tell whom you should contact by watching or listening to daily news programs, call the station and ask someone in the news department.

Friends for Keeps

Of course face-to-face meetings are always best, because less gets lost in translation when people look into each other's eyes. However, the hectic pace of daily news deadlines will require the use of the telephone or mail to convince reporters to set up personal interviews. This should not trouble you; most information carried through the media usually passes via phone or mail.

Maintaining friendships among members of the press involves common courtesies and conscientious understanding of their daily duties. Get to know all the kinds of stories your press friend covers, not just the stories about your group. Perhaps you can suggest other items outside the world of gardens, especially because people in your garden group will be active in many areas of local business and politics.

You may need to fill in the background or refresh your press friend's memory if you haven't contacted each other for a while. Remember to always follow up with any information you promise. And don't get upset if your press friend is suddenly abrupt. Deadlines sometimes make snappy brutes of even the friendliest journalist.

Above all, never let press friends down by allowing important news from your garden to escape their attention, while someone else reports it. Journalists hate to be scooped on a story they're close to. If it happens, friendly press relations could be threatened. Indeed, this will be difficult to prevent unless your group takes precautions. Seed members and gardeners should know to refer all press inquiries to the project leader or contact person, who has assumed responsibility for press coverage. This way, your press friend can be informed when other journalists express an interest in the garden.

Who Needs to Advertise?

No garden project needs to advertise, but some groups have done so. Why should they pay for ad space when they can get free coverage in local news columns and public service announcements? The answer lies in matters of emphasis. For groups that can afford it, advertising is seen as a way to determine more directly how the image of their garden project is conveyed to the public. People who advertise can control the content of their messages, while people in the news cannot. Sometimes advertising may be seen as part of a bigger public relations campaign.

Some projects with big budgets sometimes spend money on advertising. Although this looks nice, it's a needless expense, especially for neighborhood projects.

Only large community garden groups need to consider advertising, and usually just those groups that are dissatisfied with media coverage through other channels. In all cases, garden groups should not hesitate to inquire about special rates for public service organizations.

Some groups also consider another kind of advertising — want ads. These can be inexpensive and helpful when the group needs something specific, like a used Rototiller or pipe for a water main.

The Parade Route

Probably the loudest way to attract attention and drum up support is to launch a cross-town parade. The annual garden parade in Richmond, California, is held in the spring to coincide with planting season and opening of the garden. Each year's parade involves a theme and much media ballyhoo beforehand.

Lots of people in Richmond obviously love to strut. Forty organizations joined the march during the second year. These included school bands, military marching units, fifty horses, one bicycle, one stagecoach, and fifteen floats sponsored by business and civic clubs. In addition, Dr. Grow (Rev. Richard Dodson) led the parade in his Growmobile.

Dr. Grow is known around Richmond, California, for his overalls
and his Growmobile, which he
drives around town advocating
"planned planthood" and
drumming up support for the
Richmond Community Garden
Program. Dr. Grow is also Rev.
Richard Dodson, pastor of
Seaport Baptist Church. The
Growmobile and Dr. Grow
highlight the annual Richmond
Garden Parade, a major outreach effort held each spring.

How did it all start? Cora Orr and Robert Hayes, coordinators of the garden project, went directly to city hall and passed out fruit and flowers to the city council, its staff, and citizens in the chambers. "Then after they'd eaten the fruit and smelled the flowers," Robert said, "we made our request for the parade."

After that, promoting the parade was easy. A press friend helped announce and plan the event. Parade invitation forms were printed in the local newspaper. The forms asked for the names of sponsors, size of marching units, and number of people or animals involved. This information was then compiled to help planners organize the march coherently.

Getting the parade permit was perhaps the easiest task of all. Orr and Hayes simply asked the chief of police if he wanted to ride shotgun on the stagecoach. Enthusiastically, he said he did and the police department's community relations division provided the permit, no questions asked.

Parade judges sat in a review stand and awarded prizes for best marching band, sharpest drill team, best groomed horses, and most creative float. "We made a show for them," Cora said with a smile.

Aid First and Money Matters

EVENTUALLY ANY GARDEN group will have to grapple with one very basic question: Does the project need money to operate or not? This may lead to windy arguments within the seed group. How the group answers this essential question will depend on factors stretching beyond the horizon of the group's influence. Foremost among these factors is the ability of the neighborhood and community to donate land, materials, human energy, and other necessary sorts of support. Likewise, the answer depends upon realities and the abilities of people in the seed group — how open and insightful they are to determining and scavenging the things they need.

As with any public endeavor, money always involves parallel questions of free time and its value to those asking the questions. Nowhere is the diversity of approaches to vacant-lot gardening more evident than with matters of money and ongoing support. Two diametrically different examples from New York State illustrate this point. New York City's young Cooperative Extension Garden Program, sponsored through Cornell University, operates with a stupendous budget of five hundred thousand dollars — all of which is funneled into the city through a special grant from the U.S. Department of Agriculture. In contrast, in Syracuse, the four-year-old Adopt-a-Lot Program casually functions on a budget of zero dollars.

As Michael Phillips points out in his wise book, *The Seven Laws of Money,* legal tender has its own rules for keeping records, budgets, savings, and loans. How your group adheres to these rules ultimately depends on how

All during its existence, the garden will require other material goods besides seeds. Keep your eyes open for any items needed from the checklist below. Shop among friends, want ads, Salvation Army Stores, and dumps. Or find someone who will donate them.

For composting and mulching: manure, sawdust, straw, leaves, wood chips, stable sweepings, lawn clippings, other biodegradable materials. Also wheelbarrows, carts, buckets.

For planting and transplanting: hoes, rakes, shovels, spades, trowels, weeders, other tools, pots, and planters.

For defining garden spaces: wooden stakes, building wood, fencing, gate, lock and keys, wire, buckets, water pipe and fittings, hoses and nozzles.

For future possibilities: bulletin board, picnic tables and chairs, playground equipment, clear fiber glass or plastic, old windows, old tires, shed.

There's always something else.

it decides to organize and account for itself. It could go from the extreme of coaxing a local agency into covering money matters to the opposite extreme of establishing a nonprofit corporation that blankets itself.

Money for What?

No one can have good enough reasons to spend energy chasing money that isn't really needed for establishing and maintaining the garden. In order to wisely determine its abilities and needs to find funding, the seed bunch must first decide how it expects to use the money.

The group's money person and resource person must work together at this stage. Both of them need to keep one fact foremost in mind — just about everything a neighborhood garden needs may be donated to the project or found nearby. That is, if discarded materials and responsive donors can be located without an unreasonable expenditure of time. Most garden projects will require:

Land. A lease or other arrangement for long-term use and territorial trappings, including windbreaks, fence, gate, lock, and enough keys for everyone. Groups rarely buy the land they garden upon. Those that do must account for property taxes.

Soil. Acquiring and transporting manure, mulch materials, finished compost, fertilizers, or soil amendments such as granite dust and phosphate rock. Plowing or tilling expenses. Hand tools for soil preparation and cultivation.

Water. Hoses and nozzles, unless rains can be relied upon. Pipe and fittings, if none exist at the site. Water bills may be a problem in areas with drought and heavy fines for overuse.

Outreach. Printing for posters, handbills, newsletters. Photocopies. Postage or bulk mail permits. Phone.

Salaries. Biggest expense in most garden budgets, unless the project is run by volunteers. Travel expenses.

Insurance. Costs depend on coverage and carrier. Need depends on landowner, gardeners, and group sponsors. Still a nebulous area. Groups must seriously shop for the best insurance.

Extras. Playground equipment, phone-answering machine, sign painting, paved parking areas, other niceties and contingencies.

Budget Business

After a seed group determines why it needs money and how the funds are to be generally spent, the money person should draft an itemized budget. Then, together with everyone else in the group, time and concentration should be applied to decisions about where and how to begin the funding search. The group should not allow this process to drag out. Otherwise, as the garden gets going, seed group members will be caught paying out of their own pockets for printing, postage, gas, telephone, and other minor expenses. Sooner or later this inefficiency will cause headaches and dissension.

Ann Arbor's Project Grow is a good example of a small, city garden program that started as a volunteer effort and slowly grew to eight gardens with a salaried director and part-time site coordinators. Aside from salaries, Project Grow's major operating expenses in 1977 were $1,400 for plowing and tilling; $736 for water and irrigation systems; $725 for printing and photocopying; $614 for garden site expenses, including soil improvements; $544 for insurance; $500 for a telephone-answering machine; and $350 for postage and bulk mail permits.

Money to meet expenses came primarily from these sources: $6,381 from fees and donations, $5,000 from the city council, $3,495 from a HUD block grant, and $2,000 from Washtenaw County.

Professionals and Volunteers

Unquestionably, the heftiest budget item for most community garden programs is salaries. San Jose, California, budgets $138,000 annually for its innovative recreational garden program, and the city spends $48,000 of that total — over a third — for its staff of coordinators, assistants, office and garden workers, instructors, and consultants. More than two-thirds of Ann Arbor's $18,000 budget goes to paychecks for garden coordinators and a project director.

Any project with more than a couple of small garden sites will probably require at least one salaried staff member, probably the project leader. A program with several sites or one large garden will demand too much professional coordination to run entirely on volunteer efforts.

BLOCK GRANTS

Several garden coordinators say this program causes more bother and paperwork than it's worth, including lots of public hearings and an involved process that can get necessarily political. The Department of Housing and Urban Development (HUD) administers block grants directly through a city's chief executive officer, usually the mayor.

Funds for local programs are allocated after a lengthy series of agency requests, preliminary proposals, budget submissions, public hearings, further proposals, and approval of loan officers, as well as HUD.

Block grant categories relevant to community gardens include open space, neighborhood and public facilities, water and sewer facilities. Cities vying for block grant money become eligible after submission and approval by HUD of three detailed studies: 1. a three-year community development plan, 2. an annual community development program, 3. a housing assistance plan.

To determine the agency responsible for local block grant proposals, contact your mayor or nearest HUD office. Or write: Office of Community Development Programs, HUD, 451 Seventh Street SW, Washington, D. C. 20410.

No matter how large its paid staff, however, any garden project at various times will need to rely on the vital resources of unpaid volunteers. As with any civic effort involving volunteers, the staff must expect to treat them more than fairly for giving their valuable time and energy.

Insured Risks

Undoubtedly, insurance coverage is the murkiest of all items in community garden budgets. To say that the situation is confusing would be a sweeping understatement.

Some garden projects pay more than five hundred dollars a year for insurance, although no one has ever filed a claim. Others insure gardeners at minimal costs through the same plan that covers city employees in the area. Some programs require landowners to provide coverage for gardeners, while others insure the landowners against possible claims by gardeners. Another project protects itself against obligation, while gardeners are left to assume their own liability. Some programs provide coverage for bodily injury and property damage similar to auto policies; in fact they use the same forms. Elsewhere gardeners are required to sign "hold harmless" agreements drawn up by attorneys to protect landowners and program leaders. Other projects leave insurance decisions entirely up to individual groups at individual sites. And some gardens carry no insurance at all.

"We have yet to really straighten out our insurance," said Susan O'Neill of the San Francisco Community Garden Project. "This is partly because of shifting garden sites, but mostly because our 4-H coverage stipulates that each garden be classified as a 4-H Club. That means the gardens are mainly children oriented, which they are not, except for school gardens. So we are covered rather precariously."

Insurance can becloud grand plans for expansion. At Ann Arbor's spacious county farm site, which supports 180 families with many children, gardeners wanted to install playground equipment and picnic tables to enhance the site. "But the insurance agent said he would consider that a nuisance factor and it would increase our premium," said Susan Drake, one of the original Project

Grow founders. "So we had to cut out those types of things from our plans."

All these difficulties and contradictions are rooted in the fact that most insurance carriers are unfamiliar with community gardening. Most programs are not old enough to provide a history that companies can use for assessing policies.

Aetna, which insures Ann Arbor, Atlanta, and other programs, classifies neighborhood gardeners as "leasing farmers." Rates are fixed accordingly, although gardeners do not face nearly the same risks as farmers do.

Obviously, more time is needed before classifications, coverage, and rates can become reasonable and standardized. Seed groups would be wise to shop around for the best coverage at the fairest rates and to enlist the advice of a knowledgeable insurance person that everyone can trust. Obviously, the best policy would cover gardeners, as well as landowners, group members, and the project itself.

Fees for Plots

An annual fee is charged by many urban garden projects for the right to plant a plot. Fees are considered equivalent to membership dues, and they provide a major source of revenue. However, projects in Atlanta, New York, San Francisco, Newark, New Jersey, and some other cities charge no fees. Those who assess fees say it assures that people are interested and will make a commitment to maintain their plot throughout the season. Those who don't charge, say that fees are an unnecessary bookkeeping expense.

Should your group charge a fee? It depends on several factors, foremost of which is the ability of people in the neighborhood to pay. The number of anticipated gardeners is also a major factor. Will the amount of money generated make it worth the effort to collect and account for the fees? Other factors are how the seed group anticipates using fee money and what the gardeners will be offered in return for their payment.

What is a fair fee? The range spreads from twenty-five dollars to one dollar a year. In some places, seniors and low-income families are offered reduced rates. In Indianapolis, the Mayor's Garden Program offers a spacious

COOPERATION AND INCORPORATION

Most neighborhood garden groups attempt to exist on cooperation. If money is handled, it is usually diverted through a sponsoring agency that is established to account for funds, especially at tax time.

In rare cases, a garden group may decide to incorporate, to become a nonprofit, tax-exempt corporation. Gardeners at San Francisco's Fort Mason Garden incorporated primarily to handle money from an anticipated bicentennial award.

Incorporating has several advantages. Groups can hold property and thus own the garden site. They can incur debts, sue or be sued, and qualify for reduced bulk mail privileges. But the main advantage is the legal ability to handle their own money for special projects, such as demonstration sites, greenhouses, community canneries.

To incorporate, three or more people must meet, give themselves a name, elect a board of directors, draft bylaws and articles of association. Then, if the state has an income tax, the group must apply to the Franchise Tax Board as well as the Secretary of State, or equivalent officer. If the group qualifies at the state level, then it must file Internal Revenue Service (IRS) forms with the federal government.

Usually, incorporating requires the services of an attorney everyone can trust. This was no problem at Fort Mason because, among its ranks, the group included more than one lawyer.

LAND AND WATER CONSERVATION

Administered by the young and energetic Bureau of Outdoor Recreation, the Land and Water Conservation Fund (LWCF) is meant to increase everyone's opportunity for recreation outdoors. In some states, this has been interpreted to mean community gardens, as well as more standard recreation activities.

All LWCF money is allocated differently, state to state. Funds are matched, fifty-fifty, by the state liaison office, which usually determines where and how the money is spent. However, each project must meet five federal guidelines: the garden 1. must not displace existing recreation, 2. must prove that it's a needed form of recreation, 3. membership must be open to all, 4. food from the plots cannot be sold, and 5. the project must be accessible to other forms of transportation besides cars. LWCF money cannot be used for operation or maintenance of the garden.

To qualify for LWCF, a community garden program must be sponsored by a local government agency and hold a minimum five-year lease at its sites. For more information contact your state liaison officer, usually the head of the state Department of Parks and Recreation or Natural Resources. If you can't find your state liaison officer, contact the nearest BOR regional office in Philadelphia, Atlanta, Ann Arbor, Albuquerque, Denver, San Francisco, or Seattle.

plot of one thousand square feet for three dollars to anyone over sixty-five. In most cases, fee schedules are staggered depending on the size of plots. An annual charge of ten dollars for five hundred square feet seems average and equitable.

The Pennsylvania Horticulture Society's Program, in Philadelphia, has a unique system that may work in your neighborhood. It charges a steep twenty-five dollars for the first year, then nothing else thereafter. The idea of a high initial fee is to separate serious long-term gardeners from those who are not-so-sure.

A Civil Friend

No matter where your seed bunch plants itself, it will eventually have to deal with a government agency — local, state, or federal. Agencies with big acronymic names may seem ominous and inhuman. These graphic images make it difficult to visualize the people who work behind the initials of the name. These are real people, who daily interpret what the agency stands for and what it should be doing with its influence and resources.

These people answer phones, write letters, and make large or small decisions that affect the lives of many people and other forms of life. Some of these "civil servants" are genuinely committed to making their agency do what it can to create a better world, no matter how ridiculous or callous the agency looks in print and in gossip. Many are sensitive, responsible, kind people who may have kids or keep cats. Some of them may help your garden, if your group is prepared to ask.

A big part of any seed group's effort will be to find the right people in the right places in government. Searching for them can take time and more than a little effort. But someday you may find a big ally in a governmental agency that you previously considered unresponsive.

Local Support

The first place to begin looking for financial and material assistance is at home — your neighborhood, your city, your county. All kinds of local people may be willing and able to help your project. It just depends on how receptive local leaders and groups are to interpreting and including your effort in their ongoing plans for community action.

Most city and county governments own land that is unused and sometimes suitable for gardens. Contact the tax assessor or planning commission to locate tax-defaulted properties and other lands held by your local government.

Money is also available locally for specific community improvements. San Jose, California, has used capital improvement funds for preparing soil and installing permanent irrigation systems on its recreational garden sites. Ann Arbor's City Council has dipped into its general fund to assist Project Grow, and the council eventually added the energetic project as a line item in its park and recreation budget.

County government agencies have also been tapped by garden groups for specific favors and contributions. Besides school, recreation, public works, and Cooperative Extension, many community gardeners have found friends and supporters among social service agencies, health departments, county fairgrounds commissions, and community colleges.

Local quasi-political groups can also assist gardeners. These include Boy and Girl Scouts, 4-H Clubs, YMCA, YWCA, and civic groups like Odd Fellows, Kiwanis, Elks, Lions, and others established to serve the community. Also, garden centers, church groups, neighborhood improvement associations, student ecology action groups, tenant associations, welfare rights groups, and environmental councils may find ways to help your cause.

All a seed group needs to do is determine how these organizations may be able to help, then politely ask them to do so. For most of them, community service is their only reason for being.

State Aid

A few state governments have been instrumental in helping communities establish garden programs. However, the assistance has come primarily in the form of resources, not funding.

Pennsylvania began its "anti-inflation" garden program in 1975 after a proclamation by its governor, Mil-

OLDER AMERICANS ACT

The Department of Health, Education, and Welfare (HEW) has an Office of Human Development that administers the Older Americans Act, which has the potential for assiting community garden groups working with senior citizens. However, few groups have tapped into this resource.

Money from this act could be made available to groups through two areas: nutrition services and employment. In gardens, senior citizens could provide more healthful and nutritious meals, and they could be employed as master gardeners.

The State Office of Aging disburses Older Americans Act funds locally. If you can't find your local representative, contact the Office of Human Development, Administration on Aging, Department of Health, Education, and Welfare, North Building, 330 Independence Avenue SW, Washington, D. C. 20201.

EXPANDED FOOD AND NUTRITION EDUCATION

The Department of Agriculture's Expanded Food and Nutrition Education Program (EFNEP) has provided the most generous federal funding of community gardens so far. In 1977, New York alone received five hundred thousand dollars in EFNEP funds specifically for community garden use.

Philadelphia, Detroit, Chicago, Houston, and Los Angeles have also received large EFNEP grants for gardens. These cities are being watched closely to see if the money can be developed into an ongoing and active local program.

The purpose of EFNEP is to help families learn how to improve their health and eating habits. EFNEP also offers educational services that can be tapped by local community gardeners.

The program is administered locally by farm and home advisors of the county Cooperative Extension. Proposals for EFNEP funds should begin with the local county agent. If you don't know your local agent, call the nearest federal information center.

ton Shapp. Many of the gardens were planted on unused parcels of abandoned state dairy farms. In addition to land, the innovative program provided seeds and organizational advice. Coordinated through a special office of the state's Department of Agriculture, the program also involved several other branches of state government, including education, public welfare, general services, and community affairs.

Connecticut has a similar statewide program established by state law. It, too, is administered through the agriculture department. Massachusetts, through its land-use division, and California, through its parks and recreation department, also have offered limited support for community gardens in those states.

Any seed group with connections or influence in the state capitol could attempt to muster state support among various agencies besides agriculture, land use, park and recreation, general services, and the governor's office. Perhaps you can find supporters in the areas of health, natural resources, education, office of aging, youth corps for conservation or ecology, transportation, even the legislature. Some of these folks might be gardeners themselves.

Federal Funds

"Because community gardens involve health, education, welfare, agriculture, recreation, almost everything, there is hardly a grant program in the federal government that can't be converted in some way into helping these projects." The speaker is Peter Brand of the Bureau of Outdoor Recreation's (BOR) Pacific Southwest Regional Office.

Brand counts at least seven existing federal sources capable of funding garden projects. The Expanded Food and Nutrition Education Program (EFNEP), administered through the U.S. Department of Agriculture, and the Cooperative Extension Service are the largest sources of revenue for community gardening. However, many cities and counties have used the Comprehensive Employment Training Act (CETA) and the Community Food and Nutrition Program (CFNP) to bolster the budgets of garden projects. To a lesser extent the BOR's Land and Water Conservation Fund, HEW's Older Americans Act,

HUD block grants and ACTION minigrants have been used to assist urban and neighborhood gardeners.

Each of these programs has its own regulations and limitations. Also, programs change as administrations change. So the seed bunch needs to know someone close to the federal government, who can help keep tabs on new developments in funding, including congressional acts. Even then, Brand offers these words of warning:

"I'm well aware that the federal government is a mixed blessing. And grant programs are often a lot more trouble than they're worth, particularly when you're talking about small-scale solutions like community gardens. A lot of community gardeners have said, 'I wish we hadn't done it...we wasted more time than it was worth trying to figure out and administer the program.' So I caution you, if you're thinking about government money, think twice before getting involved in a federal grant program."

Doing Without Money

Two most active examples of garden programs that have been initiated and maintained without budgets can be found in Richmond, California, and Syracuse, New York. In both cases, coordinators chose to use neighborhood and local resources and services instead of pursuing state, federal, and other wellsprings of funding.

Syracuse's Adopt-a-Lot is supported by Cooperative Extension, professional societies, the board of realtors, supermarkets, a tractor company, garden clubs, garden stores, colleges, farmers, and even a hotel. All are frequently credited in publications distributed by the garden coordinators.

Richmond's program survives with the same thirst for community input. A total of thirteen community groups and neighborhood improvement associations joined to help launch the project. Also, numerous city and county government agencies offered their resources.

"We figured that people like the City Council, the Parks Department, the county Cooperative Extension, and so forth would help us if we didn't ask for money," said Robert Hayes. "So that's what we did. We asked for services...which actually equalled a lot more than it would have in cash value."

COMPREHENSIVE EMPLOYMENT AND TRAINING

Some cities — notably Honolulu, Los Angeles, and San Francisco — have been able to use Department of Labor statistics and funds from the Comprehensive Employment and Training Act (CETA) to provide jobs for people in community garden related activities. Jobs include tasks like hauling manure and mixing compost, as well as administrative chores. Some CETA people assist gardeners with guidance and educational information.

Allocation of CETA funds is based on the unemployment statistics of an area. Mostly it's an urban program, with counties of over one hundred thousand population drawing most of the money. The more jobless people in a city, the more potential CETA workers. However, CETA does have monies for counties under the one hundred thousand population figure. These "balance of state" counties are ranked according to current unemployment figures. A state government office, usually the governor's, divides the money proportionately among the less-populated counties.

The purpose of CETA is stated in the title: employment and training. But local agencies determine how the funds are to be distributed. The Labor Department considers the local agency the "prime sponsor" for CETA. If you are unsure who, in your county, is prime sponsor, contact the nearest Department of Labor regional office (Boston, New York, Philadelphia, Atlanta, Chicago, Dallas, Kansas City, Denver, San Francisco, or Seattle). They should be able to help you find where CETA money goes in your community. Or write the Employment and Training Administration of the Department of Labor, 601 D Street NW, Room 5402, Washington, D. C. 20213.

COMMUNITY FOOD AND
NUTRITION

The purpose of the Community
Food and Nutrition Program
(CFNP) is ". . . to reduce the in-
cidence of hunger and malnutri-
tion among the poor and to improve their nutritional status." A
program of the Community Services Administration, CFNP also
develops self-help and alternative
food production and distribution
methods.

Groups eligible to apply for CFNP
funds are county Community
Action agencies, migrant and seasonal farmworker organizations.
Others are Indian organizations,
tribal governments, other public
or private nonprofit organizations
and agencies that meet Community Services Administration (CSA)
eligibility standards.

Community garden programs
fit under the "self-help projects"
category. These projects are
"designed to foster self-sufficiency through the mobilization
of financial and community resources as well as the inclusion
of the poverty community in
their development and imple-
mentation." Funds are used to
plan and establish projects according to CSA guidelines. However, other sources of ongoing
support must be enlisted.

CSA maintains regional offices
in Boston, New York, Philadelphia, Atlanta, Chicago, Dallas,
Kansas City, Denver, San Francisco, and Seattle. If they can't
help you find the name of your
local Community Action agency,
contact CSA, 1200 19th St. NW,
Washington, D. C. 20506.

Done with Wits

Any project that exists without money needs to operate on a balanced account of wits. Seed people need to have their feelers stretched throughout local communities for aid of all sorts. Anything that costs money (fencing, irrigation systems, wood and glass for cold frames) may be donated, if you find a willing donor. Those who give charitably to civic projects are usually well aware of the tax breaks involved.

"You don't need to go out and buy a lot of stuff," Hayes said. "Someone in the city has got it, and it's not being used. They just don't know how to go about getting it to you.

"So what you have to do is create a way for them to be useful. You don't just go in and say 'I want you to give me this stuff.' You say, 'Look, it would be helpful if you let us use some of the materials you're not using.' Then they say, 'Well I don't know how.' And you say, 'Well maybe if you did it this way.' Then they come around."

Of course, Hayes doesn't stop there.

"Whenever someone gives us something," he said, "we try our best to get it into the newspaper. If it's in the paper, then they really are happy."

Independence and Sourcefulness

Innovative programs blend donations of materials with funding from a diversity of sources. Except for long-term use of land, almost everything a garden needs can be gotten for free or cheaply. However, many people are not inclined to expend the effort required by scavenger hunting and bargain shopping. They would rather spend their energy searching for funding. In all cases, seed people must commit themselves to a thorough search of community sources and resources.

A true sense of independence depends on how small the project can remain without relying too much on support from civic groups, government agencies, and absentee contributors far beyond the neighborhood. Getting what you want, when you want it, always involves reliance on others to a certain extent. But a good way to avoid over-dependence on a single source is to set strict limitations on the number of times a source can be tapped. Do this before the limitations begin to establish themselves and a once brimming fountain of aid quickly dries up.

Any thriving neighborhood garden is composed entirely of willing individuals who can trust themselves and others to accomplish what they set out to do. But these people must also realize that the entire effort is well beyond the abilities of any of them as individuals. The blooming truths of any garden are established by guiding forces far greater than the singular strengths of active individuals.

Matters of Attitude

Whether a garden project runs on money or sweat is actually beside the point. Rather, a positively undaunted attitude on the part of those who lead the project has more to do with its success than balanced budgets or non-monetary matters of community etiquette.

Lee Tecklenburg expresses this attitude very well. Tecklenburg, a responsive and cordial coordinator of Sacramento County's Cooperative Extension program in California, goes to great lengths to decipher the strengths and resources in his home town, which is also the state capital.

"I really have to work to educate myself," Lee said. "I attend every seminar I can, and I'm involved in every political campaign. I deal with real estate people, and I know where the money is in town. I know who controls what. I deal on the broadest base I possibly can."

He also knows the proper cords to pull with local and state government agencies that have something to offer the gardens. It works for him because he knows "bureaucracy isn't really all that difficult."

But the real key to Sacramento's gardening successes is carried in Tecklenburg's understanding of how people are ultimately moved to accomplish big tasks together.

"I don't want to hear anyone say we can't do it," he said. "I just want to know what we want done. Then we'll just figure out how to get it done."

ACTION

A sort of domestic Peace Corps, ACTION offers small grants-in-aid to nonprofit community volunteer groups. A few of these mini-grants have gone to community garden projects.

The grants are intended to get projects rolling. However, this seed money is usually restricted to environmental, women's and Indians' issues. Few grants exceed five thousand dollars, and they are spent mostly on salaries, supplies, and other tools.

Local groups must make a "preliminary inquiry" with the state ACTION office. This is then sent to Washington, where ACTION agents determine if they want to see a full proposal.

ACTION has ten regional offices —Boston, New York, Philadelphia, Atlanta, Chicago, Dallas, Kansas City, Denver, San Francisco, Seattle — as well as state and division offices. Check a phone book. For more information, contact the Director of Information Collection and Exchange, Office of Multilateral and Special Programs, ACTION, 806 Connecticut Avenue, Washington, D. C. 20525.

Lee Tecklenburg

3
PLACES

Plenty of Lots

VACANT LOTS are everywhere, in every city and every town. Much of this vacant land is created by the economic and tax realities of a neighborhood. Some vacant land is created by geography. Many lots are available for use as gardens. There are many possible terms for land use, including leases, rents, and squatting. The more permanent the land-use agreement, the bolder the garden can grow. People should learn to discriminate. Lots of land is available.

Some vacant lots near city centers, like this one in Boston's North End, are often too small and too shaded for gardens. No more than a couple of families can garden here; and buildings block the sun, so their choices of what to grow are limited too. Besides, it's also a busy neighborhood with lots of tourists. A garden might be better located on a rooftop around here.

In Europe, garden plots are often alloted along railroad right-of-ways. Community gardens aren't found along tracks in America very often. However, if a parcel isn't in too grimy a spot, you may want to consider it.

Unused areas of parks have provided the best spots for gardens in some communities. Here a garden can be big enough to accommodate more than a hundred families. Besides, parkland is already cleared and preserved. Care should be taken to locate any garden away from smokestacks and heavy industry or areas that have been compacted by automobile traffic.

The best spots for gardens in many neighborhoods are small lots, the size of single-family-home plots. In most cities these lots range from 50 to 100 feet to 75 by 150 feet. Depending on how the group chooses to divide it, two to eight families could garden a lot this size. Corner lots get more sun and wind exposure — and more traffic. The garden plan should always consider these factors.

Weeds can help you tell if a vacant lot is a good spot for a garden. A broad diversity of weeds from many families growing in a vacant lot usually indicates that a broad variety of garden plants will also grow there. How many different families of weeds do you see at the sites you're considering?

Some lots are full of rock, gravel, and rubbish. They're so much trouble to clean up that these lots are probably best left vacant. Some places are just too difficult to transform into a garden.

Big sunny lots with room for over a dozen gardeners are not hard to find in some neighborhoods. This is especially true in areas where commercial zoning creates parcels larger than single-family-residential lots. But these areas also have more thoroughfares, more activity, more noise, and more mess. Boy and Girl Scouts, 4-H Clubs, and youth conservation groups may be enlisted to help your group clean up a community garden site. As long as they can show that it was educational experience, kids will get points for badges and awards.

A Common
Place to Begin

SELF-FULFILLING PLACES that modern people have come to
know as neighborhood and community gardens are not
random experiments upon the face of the earth. In light
of human uses of land, they are indeed based on long-
standing precedents of stewardship and respect for natural systems. These traditional ideas can be traced through
the slow evolution of many cultures and agricultures.

Because food is always a common need in all times and
places, people have been prone to fill that need by acting
together. However, the modern view of land and people's
place upon it is beclouded by machines and their power
to strip and masticate land. This view is further obfus-
cated by the concept of private property: self-possession
of something that no one can reproduce — the land, the
soil, the life that grows upon and within it.

To better comprehend the place of community gardens
in the evolution of human beings, it is again necessary to
dip into history. We must wander back to England and
the British "open field" or "common field" system.
During the Middle Ages, land around an English village
was essentially one common farm. Villagers worked
together in unfenced fields. The village owned the plow
and individuals provided the energy to motivate it. Land
belonged to everyone and no one, at once. Fields grew
wheat, rye, barley, oats, peas, and beans. Or they stood
fallow, all this in a predetermined seasonal rotation of
crops.

DANISH GARDEN COLONIES

Individual orchards, gardens, and animal pens were enclosed. Lowlands were left open for meadow and pasture. The remaining lands — the heaths, bogs, thickets, forests — were left to "waste." This means they supplied peat for fuel and wood, sand, gravel, and humus for home and land maintenance. They also gave additional grazing space for cattle when they could not feed in pastures, fields, or other village grounds. Any such so-called wasteland was known as the commons.

The open-field system worked for several centuries. But as population slowly increased on the small island, British food production demanded a more controlled land base. Farms began counting their worth in bushels of corn instead of in community cooperation. In 1709, Parliament passed the first of a series of enclosure acts that fenced fields and closed commons. Slowly the landscape began to change. These acts continued to be mandated for 160 years before people finally realized that growing cities were creating problems that could not be solved by acquiring more land or enclosing more commons. The British people were beginning to appreciate the value of commons purely as open space, as a break from the monotony of fenced crops and uninterrupted rows of houses.

Overseas Allotments

Later, open space began to mean more than wild and tumbled places. Early in the nineteenth century, English cities and towns were required by law to set aside garden land for the poor and unemployed. These gardens were for recreation and food production. Germany, Switzerland, and Sweden began similar programs. The custom spread to Austria, Belgium, France, Luxembourg, Holland, Denmark. It became known as the allotment garden system, and it continues to this day.

Many people who visit Europe marvel at the allotment gardens. "It seems that every little parcel of land around cities is being used for growing vegetables and flowers," reported James W. Wilson of the National Garden Bureau. "Many of these gardens have a two- and three-year waiting period, and some leases have been held for so long that people have constructed beautiful little tool sheds modeled after chalets and summer cabins."

Other island nations have gardens similar to the allotment gardens of Europe. "You drive in Japan or Indoesia, and you see they use every available square foot, right up to the edge of the road. It's all used to grow something because you know there's very little land," said Calvin Hamilton of the Los Angeles City Planning Department. "From a city planning point of view, it's important to put vacant land to work like this."

Liberty and Victory Gardens

American community gardens developed along different lines. During the beginning of the Industrial Revolution, factories set aside land for employee gardens. School children learned, at the turn of the century, how to garden in neighborhood parks. Cleveland still has a school garden program that traces its roots back to 1904. The program was extensively revised in the early 1930s; it has become a model for other cities that are planning community and youth garden programs through their local school systems. Behind one Cleveland school spreads a five-and-a-half acre garden that has been producing vegetables, flowers, and young gardeners for over fifty years.

In 1918, during the First World War, Americans were asked to join a Liberty Garden Campaign. Gardeners were told how they could support soldiers by growing vegetables. However, the program was poorly organized and confusion clouded the effort. Many gardeners were frustrated by poor results in hastily prepared plots. The war ended before the campaign could impress anyone.

The Victory Garden Program of World War II was more successful. An estimated forty million people were involved. Like the British "Dig for Victory" gardens, the program was spurred by rationing and public support for the war effort. However, American victory gardens were never threatened by bombs, like their British counterparts. Many acres of vacant land were brought into production in cities and on farms. It didn't matter who you were. Farmers, backyard gardeners, senior citizens, children all got involved. Anyone who could grow vegetables was asked to join, and vacant lots that weren't producing were ordered cleared and kept neat anyway.

WHAT MADE A GOOD VICTORY GARDEN?

The Cooperative Extension Service was the kingpin of the Victory Garden Program. It coordinated the nationwide effort through its county extension agents. According to the Extension Service, a good victory garden followed these guidelines:

1. It was located nearby, so gardeners could walk to it.

2. The soil did not flood or erode.

3. The site faced south and east for the most sun.

4. Direct sunlight filled the garden for at least half of the day.

5. Gardeners avoided planting near factories or smokestacks.

6. Soil was kept deep, fertile, and "sweet."

7. Any size place or odd spot was used to grow food.

Year-round victory gardening was encouraged, so were canning, drying, and other forms of food storage. Neighborhood block leaders, tutored by the USDA Cooperative Extension Service, helped keep gardeners informed and their gardens productive. Laws and stiff penalties were passed against vandalizing or stealing from the gardens. Many gardens had flags planted in them as a reminder of the fight overseas.

After the war, victory gardens were mostly forgotten amid victory celebrations and promises of prosperity. But at least one of these gardens has survived to this day. Boston's Fenway Garden began in 1942, six months after bombs fell on Pearl Harbor. The garden is located on a wild five acres of open space near Fenway Park, home of the Boston Red Sox. The Fenway gardeners have been organized into a nonprofit society for many years, and they have withstood attempts to develop the valuable land into parking lots, schools, and hospitals.

Finding Common Ground

Mechanical means of feeding people run against the grain of history. Petrochemical energy now determines the choices and prices of food more than do human factors. But people don't need to be left out of the productive side of this absurd equation. Neighborhood and community gardens can bring it all back into balance by bringing it closer to home.

Garden Insight

THROUGH ITS OUTREACH EFFORTS, the group will have determined the demand for a garden and introduced potential gardeners to the best intentions of the project. The next step is to start a serious search for vacant lots that make the most sense as potential sites.

Check with local planning or zoning commissions to learn if restrictions prohibit the use of specific parcels or if any projected use for the lot could hamper the garden after it is planted. Avoid selecting a garden site where proposed buildings would block sunlight and create problems, such as heavier traffic and additional noise and pollution.

Seed people and future gardeners who are interested ought to conduct an extensive survey of the neighborhood, block by block, to determine the availability of vacant land. The project leader should coordinate the effort and the garden person should help determine which lots would be good sites for the group to sink roots.

Several kinds of open places can be used for gardens, but the best are those that could become as permanent as possible. These include tax-defaulted lots, future park or open space land (especially if the garden is included in the planning stages), and surplus school property (if the garden is used occasionally for teaching).

Surplus government land, unused areas of present parks, residential vacant lots, grounds around churches and suburban office buildings, unused fringes of golf courses and small airports, and perhaps flat, sturdy rooftops with adequate access are somewhat permanent possibilities.

According to E. E. Pfeiffer, "Weeds are specialists. Having learned something in the battle for survival, they will survive under circumstances where our cultivated plants, softened through centuries of protection and breeding, cannot stand up against Nature's caprices. Weeds, then, may be grouped according to their peculiarities."

But first you must know how to identify them. Find an experienced gardener, college botanist, nursery person, or Cooperative Extension agent to help. Weeds can be grouped according to the story they tell of a soil's condition.

Previously cultivated: lamb's quarters, plantain, chickweed, purslane, buttercup, dandelion, nettle, prostrate knotweed, amaranth, ragweed, mayweed, prickly lettuce, field speedwell, mallow, carpetweed.

Sandy and poor: goldenrod, ononis, broom bush, yellow toadflax, flowered aster, sandbur.

Slightly acid: daisies, horsetails, field sorrel.

Increasingly acid and compact: sorrel, dock, horsetail, fingerleaf weed, lady's-thumb.

Very acid: hawkweed, knapweed, cinquefoil, swampy horsetail.

Hardpan: field mustard, horse nettle, morning glory, quack grass, chamomile, pennycress.

Highway, railroad, and utility right-of-ways, along with buffer zones around cemeteries and prisons can also be used. But these sites are somewhat temporary. The most temporary possibilities of all, however, are investment properties, future building sites, and unused parcels in light industrial parks.

Weeding Out Lots

Picking the perfect spot for a garden will take time. No one should rush this process. Being selective now beats feeling sorry later. The group should make an accurate and thorough inventory of local resources, as well as available lots in the neighborhood, so you can give yourselves the widest possible range of choices.

Someone, preferably the contact person, will need to keep track of these choices. But the method of record keeping should be accessible and comprehensible to everyone in the seed bunch. An old recipe box full of three by five cards is one way. Another way is to use a big topographic map from the U.S. Geological Survey or a planning department map, if you can get one.

When looking for vacant land, several criteria should be kept in mind so lots can be ranked according to their best potentials. Make note of weeds and what they say about the soil, the size of the lots and how each will suit the group's demand for space, the sun and shade that falls upon the spot, the availability of public access and water, and the direction of prevailing winds.

The leading indicator of a vacant lot's potential as a garden is the growth of weeds upon it, if any. This is the first fact to recognize, because weeds will tell the true story of the growing conditions and health of the soil.

If a lush and wide variety of weed growth is evident, you can expect the site to support a good diversity of garden life too. The presence of dandelions, plantain, amaranth, purslane, nettles, and lamb's quarters indicates previous cultivation and probably a rich topsoil.

Other weeds will tell if the soil has problems. Chamomile, morning glory, field mustard, and quack grass will signify hardpan soil which does not drain well. Goldenrod, sandbur, yellow toadflax (or butter-and-eggs) and flowering aster point out sandy soils that will not hold moisture.

The absence of weeds will indicate the poorest soils. Lots that have been compacted by heavy equipment or parking will not drain well and won't support many weeds. And if weeds can't grow there, nothing else will, without a major soil-building effort.

What else can you tell about vacant-lot soils by direct observation? Take a trowel or shovel along and dig down at least twelve inches and see. How deep, dark, crumbly, and sweet smelling is the topsoil? How hard is the subsoil? Does anyone know if water stands on the lot after a hard rain? Land with poor drainage needs an improved soil structure before most vegetables will grow there.

Room Enough

Are the vacant lots under consideration big enough for all those who intend to garden there? Will enough room be available for pathways, flower borders, common plots, picnic and rest areas? These are important questions that ultimately must be answered by everyone. But the garden person needs to make a rough working estimate of the total amount of land the group requires. This must be based on the expected needs of the potential gardeners.

There are no hard and fast rules for determining this. Some garden coordinators estimate that 20- by 20-foot plots are adequate enough for a family of four. However, this depends entirely on the kinds of food grown and the appetites of the four. For some families of four, even a 50- by 50-foot plot isn't big enough.

No one should ever expect to become self-sufficient on a community garden plot. So trade offs will be necessary. What is needed at this point is a rough working estimate for sizing up each lot you consider. This necessarily involves balancing the lot size with the expectations of the gardeners.

Sun, Shade, and Access

Ideally, the garden should be exposed to full sunlight for at least half a day. Southern exposure is best, but the lot should also be free of tall shade-producing obstacles on all sides except north. It will also be helpful to deter-

If your garden must be located near heavy industries, highways, or near any street with steady traffic, you should be very concerned about the presence of lead and other atmospheric pollutants that settle on plants and soil.

Here's one way to deal with leafy greens and the older edible parts of plants that are more exposed to auto emissions: Wash them in a bath of water and vinegar. Dry them well before preparing them for the table. Another safeguard is to grow these plants in cold-frames, cloches, or greenhouses.

LEAD WEIGHT

Lead is a poison that acts slowly on the nervous system. Over the years, lead has become widespread in the environment mostly due to its use as a gasoline additive and a base for paints.

However, humans are better able to handle lead when it's in their stomachs than they are when it's in their lungs, according to Helga Olkowski of the Integral Urban House. "The major route of lead into the body is through the lungs," said Mrs. Olkowski. "If it's too dangerous to grow vegetables there, it's too dangerous to *breathe* there!"

mine the sun's highest and lowest (solstice) points on the eastern and western horizons, so morning and afternoon light can be accounted for. If the lot has spots that are shaded during midday, these could be considered for picnic, play, and rest areas. Or they could be planted in shade-loving flowers.

Easy public access to the lot must also be provided. People should be able to enter and leave the site easily, especially if the garden is to include older and handicapped people. The best lot would be located centrally for everyone who anticipates gardening there. That way people can walk or ride a bike to their plots.

If the rains aren't reliable, a source of water must be available. Does the lot have a water main, faucets, fixtures, and a meter? Are faucets located so hoses can easily reach all plots? The longest hoses usually extend no further than seventy-five feet.

Wind is also a major factor for consideration. Do prevailing winds blow in a predictable way across the lot? Plants will need to be protected if winds are strong and gusty during the growing season. Wind can damage plants. Ask nearby gardeners, weather professionals, or neighbors about wind patterns; or watch for them yourself. Also, take note if the lot is downwind from a factory, highway, or other source of pollution.

Hidden Dangers

Greedy, unchecked technology has rendered many areas of modern life unsafe. You would have to be a scientist to be certain of the exact levels of toxicity in most spots, but common sense should tell you that some vacant lots are a poor choice for gardens.

Avoid land near major highways and expressways, where atmospheric lead and other pollutants make breathing hazardous to gardeners, as well as to plants and soil. Likewise, lots near heavy industrial areas with smokestack and water pollution should be avoided. Again, this is not only for the sake of what pollution does to the soil and plants, but also for what it does to the gardeners' well-being.

Sometimes the dangers will be very difficult to detect. For example, soils may be contaminated on sites where buildings covered with lead-based paints have been demolished and pulverized into the soil. This was the case with many sites in St. Louis, where Environmental Response, a group composed mostly of students from Washington University, discovered high levels of lead in the soil.

Another subtle danger exists in places near broadcast antennas, microwave relay stations, and radar installations. These are poor choices for garden sites because gardeners may be unduly exposed to radiation levels that could have all sorts of adverse effects on human tissue. These effects may include cataracts, nervous-system disorders, chromosome breaks, blood diseases and disorders, or possible cancer.

Siteless Spots

If your neighborhood has very little vacant land, everyone will naturally need to be less selective and more willing to use alternative methods to bring about the garden. Lots with useless soil can still be used, if people will make the extra effort required to build raised planting beds and fill them with rich soil heaped twelve to twenty-four inches above the poor existing topsoil.

Mark Malony, coordinator of gardens for Contra Costa County in California, has learned to do this because his program cannot afford to turn down land. "We can't be choosy," Mark said. "You take what you can get."

Sometimes, as in the case of the Adams-Morgan neighborhood in Washington, D.C., vacant lots are virtually nonexistent. Gil Friend of the Institute for Local Self-Reliance reports that only two acres of vacant land exist in the area, which covers less than one square mile and includes thirty to forty thousand people. However, this did not deter the institute from helping people find vacant space to garden in the neighborhood. They went to vacant roof spaces that were flat, accessible, and strong enough to support planter boxes. In Montreal, the Minimum Cost Housing Group of McGill University's School of Agriculture has established a large rooftop garden on a community center. This has provided an excellent model for those willing to garden above the crowded level of the street.

HEAVY METAL TESTING

Local government agencies should be able to help you test soils and sewage sludge, as well as garden and store produce, for dangerous accumulations of lead, cadmium, nickel, chromium, copper, zinc, and other heavy metals. Gil Friend of the Institute for Local Self-Reliance offers these suggestions for such testing.

Find an agency to provide an analysis. Try Cooperative Extension, air-quality monitors, public health agencies, or a college professor (chemistry or environmental studies) who needs a good class project.

Limit your sample. Collect from different gardens at different distances from the pollution source. Also pick "control group" samples of the same foods from a market. Gather at least five samples of each type. Keep records.

Store samples in individual plastic bags. Label. Test samples as soon as possible.

Evaluate results, usually expressed in parts per million, with the agency. Compare different crop types; compare garden and market types. Assess garden sites.

Supporting Communities

To actually transform a vacant eyesore into a productive and long-standing garden, the seed group must capture the imagination and support of agencies and organizations outside the neighborhood, as well as those within it. Support can take many forms including money, materials, services, information, and assertive introductions to people who can help you make short cuts along the way.

Most important, any seed group must recognize and respect the sometimes subtle streams of local power. No new group can barge into an existing organization's sacred territory with blatant disregard for existing structures of authority. Everyone in the seed bunch must be sensitive to this, so nobody's civic feet get stepped on. When treated with respect, local organizations and agencies will lend priceless support and influence to the garden effort when their help is most needed.

One way to awaken community interest in your project is to put together a slide show or other graphic model that fully depicts the amount of abused vacant land, the needs for the garden, and the ways the group intends to establish it. After the slide show, it's a good idea to conduct a follow-up tour of the most promising lots to enlighten and rally potential supporters.

Finding Landowners

Idle land is always owned by somebody, but that somebody is not always an individual. A promising lot could be held by a corporation, municipality, utility, church, or other entity. With an exact address or a precise location, finding the owner is a mere matter of going to the county tax assessor and consulting the tax records.

People in the assessor's office can also tell you which lots are tax-deeded properties that can be purchased for an amount usually equal to the unpaid back taxes. The assessor may have a separate delinquent tax office to handle these parcels. Idle lands held by various government agencies could be used for gardening, if you can convince the right persons in the right agency.

Acquiring land owned by cities and municipalities requires a visit to the city planning agency and an inquiry

SLIDE SHOWS

As mentioned, one way to demonstrate the wealth of idle people and vacant land in a neighborhood is to document this in a photographic slide show. Slide shows can easily be expanded to include photos of gardeners and of lots after they bloom.

If you don't have a projector, tape recorder, or other equipment, try to borrow rather than rent one. Approach churches, neighborhood associations, perhaps schools or other places with large, quiet rooms that can be darkened enough in the daytime or evening for slides to be seen. Other considerations:

Circulate posters or flyers to announce the event.

Make a taped sound track with words and music, if possible.

Don't show the slides too quickly.

Don't talk too much.

Tell complete stories with some photos and incomplete stories with others.

(opposite)
The rooftop of the St. Urbain Community Center in Montreal was transformed into a community garden by architecture students at McGill University working closely with people in the neighborhood. The rooftop proved to be a good garden spot because it has outside steps providing direct access to the playground below. By using wooden crates as planter boxes, plants were strategically placed so as not to stress the roof. Gardeners also experiment with various types of greenhouses, cold frames, and forcing structures.

(Photo courtesy McGill University Minimum Cost Housing Group)

All kinds of local institutions, associations, and agencies may be able to assist your garden effort in some way, including acquiring land, funding, free services, materials, research short cuts, and general assistance in administering the program. Learn how to see your entire community as a living wellspring of resources and information relevant to your garden. Here are some agencies to consider approaching for assistance. Perhaps your community has others. Not all will help, but it doesn't hurt to ask those that you feel may be able to aid your efforts.

Mayor's office
City manager
Local supervisor or councilperson
Zoning commission or planner
Public works department
Parks and recreation
Community development or re-
    development
Human resources and human de-
    velopment
City beautification council
School system
Civic clubs like Rotary, Kiwanis,
    Odd Fellows, Elks, Moose,
    Lions
Churches
Neighborhood improvement asso-
    ciations
Community colleges and univer-
    sities
Boy and Girl Scouts
4-H Clubs
Future Farmers of America
Farm Bureau
Property owners groups
League of Women Voters
Garden centers
Banks
Savings and loan associations
Public utilities
Small businesses and corporations
Others

about a possible variance to use the lot for gardening. You should also try the redevelopment agency, parks and recreation, board of education, city building and public works departments to determine if any of these hold vacant lands in your neighborhood. Using such land may require approval from the supervisors, city council, mayor, or city manager.

County planners may know of unused areas on county-owned park, farm, hospital, or former poorhouse land. Then you should see the appropriate agency and inquire who ultimately approves the use of these parcels.

Some states have land resources, land management, or land-use departments that account for excess state-owned real estate. See the U.S. Bureau of Land Management or Bureau of Outdoor Recreation regional offices for information about surplus federal lands.

Land Arrangements

Before anyone can settle into a garden site, the seed group must make some kind of arrangement with the owner to use the land. Also, it makes good sense to check with the planning department for zoning or other ordinances that might restrict use. If necessary, enlist the services of an attorney. If you have no budget, barter for services. Gardeners have made various types of arrangements for use of vacant lots, including:

Squatting. The owner cannot be found, so the garden is established without approval. Temporary and tenuous.

Rental. Also temporary. The gardeners are subject to eviction without notice.

Lease. Preferred by most gardeners, rather than renting for an unspecified period. Usually a token fee is involved.

Affirmative easement. Negotiated right to use land for the purpose of gardening.

Loophole lands. Tax breaks provided to landowner who donates portion of land to gardens for educational purposes. This can be done in conjunction with a community college or other institution.

Leaseback. Land acquired by purchase or gift, then leased to the group for a specific purpose.

Donation. All rights of land given to gardeners. Usually provides greatest tax break for landowners.

Land trust or park foundation. Land taken off the speculative market and legally held in stewardship by the group or other association.

Permanence or Wasted Effort

Establishing a garden for a group of people on idle land that probably has been neglected and abused will obviously involve a complex effort and timely coordination among a lot of people. When considering the use of any site, the seed bunch should concentrate its energy on permanence, settling into the spot and remaining there for as long as the garden is able to bloom for its supporters.

Leases or other arrangements should be drawn up for as long a term as possible — but no less than five years. Ultimately the group may want to look into ways of acquiring the lot, once the soil and the people prove they can support the garden. So the seed group should commit itself to remain on the spot for as long as it can. No one wants to squander energy on a half-baked project, which will eventually prove to be more wasteful than the weeds that naturally reclaim the lot from human neglect.

Mark Malony of Contra Costa County echoes the feelings of people who garden together in one place for more than one season. "A lot of people in the first couple of years ask, 'Is this garden going to be here next year? Should I invest a lot of time in the soil?' They hesitate because there's always that doubt. But after the second or third year, there's a feeling of 'Hey! We've been here. We've experienced some things, and now we're willing to put in the time and effort it takes to keep it going.' And that makes a whole lot of difference."

Sites for Sore Eyes

COMMUNITY GARDENS have been located in many kinds of odd spots, as well as some normal ones. Vacant land near churches, freeways, railroads, housing projects, farms, riverbanks and many other places have been sites for gardens.

About twenty-three families work plots in this garden (right) behind Zion Lutheran Church in Ann Arbor, Michigan. Although Ann Arbor is a spacious town, 42 percent of the residents live in apartment houses or multiple family dwellings with little space for gardening. There's enough room on the church grounds for ball fields and playgrounds, as well as the garden.

Unused campus land at the University of California, Santa Cruz, was transformed into an intensively cultivated horticultural wonderland called "The Farm" (left). This garden grew out of the influences of Alan Chadwick, a West Coast horticultural hero. The Farm demonstrated raised beds, intensive interplanting, and composting. No individual plots are held here.

Employees at Anderson Grain Storage facilities near Champaign, Illinois, have a small garden within sight of the company's extensive grain elevator system. Some years interest in the garden is slow. Other years people are more enthusiastic.

Kids have been gardening at Ben Franklin School in Cleveland, Ohio, for over half a century. Ben Franklin's garden (below) is part of the city school system's horticulture program, which began in 1904. It's the oldest and best organized youth garden program in the country. More than twenty thousand students are involved throughout the city at fourteen school sites and at home gardens.

Gardening under freeways and other highway locations may seem like a wise use of space, but hidden dangers fill the air around these gardens. Fallout of lead and other automotive exhausts is certainly deposited on this garden. Food taken from here must be carefully washed before it can be eaten.

Gardens near high-rise buildings can be hindered if the buildings block direct sunlight during much of the day. Especially avoid places where big buildings are located due south of the proposed garden site.

Long-term improvements, like wells and permanent crops, can be attempted if the garden group established a land trust or some other long-term agreement for use of the land. This garden is in Oakland.

Blooming Within Reach

AFTER A LOT HAS BEEN SELECTED and everyone is committed to develop it into as permanent a site as possible, the seed group must plan and prepare for the birds, bugs, wildlings, plants, and people that will actually grow there. This involves deliberately weaving several intricate elements:

Building fences and wind barriers to keep out inclemency, vagrants, and wildlife.

Providing a system to tap water and supply plants.

Laying out plots according to the variety of needs and space demanded of them.

Deciding how to segregate those who wish to spread chemicals from those who won't.

Establishing open space for kids and common plots for plants that thrive best in groups.

Working out a system that offers individuals an orderly way to sign up for plots or be put onto a waiting list.

Deciding, as a group, what to do ultimately about weeds that can both bedevil and benefit gardeners.

These elements all require fancy-free steps and the loose footwork necessary for creating a garden where one has never bloomed before.

Fences and Good Neighbors

Most garden projects are bothered in varying degrees by stray animals and by sneaky thieves and cowardly vandals who would be unable to say boo to a goose if anyone

Cora Orr, Richmond Garden Co-ordinator, has strong feelings about fences around community gardens. No fence surrounds the gardens in her California home town.

"If you say community garden," she said, "then you don't need a fence for security. I just feel that if you're really talking about community pride and togetherness, then you can't box people in or out. If it means boxing people out, then you haven't got a community garden."

Cora knows she's being idealistic. That doesn't stop her. "Sure somebody takes a squash, or a kid throws a tomato. But it's still. . . it's love that we're after, and sharing. It's ours, it's yours, it's everybody's. Anyway the most you're putting into it is love and care. And love is meant to be shared!

"Now that's being grandmotherly, I know, but that's just the way I believe. I saw the eastern gardens, and I saw the fences. I saw that in Hartford; I saw some in Boston and lots in New York. That's not what we wanted. In our case, the garden belongs to the people, and the work is done by the people. And since it's a people's garden, it shouldn't be fenced.

". . . I wouldn't be involved if we had to worry about fences."

ever caught them. A fence is usually the first item that seed groups consider after they have occupied their site. A fence restricts random traffic and defines the territory. Fences can become costly, but they can also be built of many unbought materials, including packing crates or other discarded wood. Although scavenged wood fences don't last long, they can always be rebuilt as long as free wood is readily available.

Other groups prefer to install a tall chain-link fence with a solid gate for security purposes. This involves the additional expense of locks and enough keys for every gardener, unless one person is responsible for locking and unlocking the garden every day at specified times.

Cats, birds, and vandals are not always stopped by fences. In fact, a fence may actually encourage some vandals. "As far as young people are concerned," says Cora Orr, "barriers are only put up for them to challenge. So it becomes a big deal — how to get over it, tear it down, break through, burn it out. I mean what's the point?"

Wind Breaks

Strong winds will howl over plants, burn leaves, and dry up soils. Gardens should be sheltered from the damaging effects of unexpected gusts and inclement gales. Some sort of protection from prevailing winds must be provided, expecially for gardens situated near lakes, bays, and oceans; under the gaps of hills and ridges; or on the Great Plains.

A garden can have two kinds of windbreaks, living and inert. Conifers, or evergreen trees and shrubs, are frequently used to block wind. Privet hedges (Ligustrum genus) are too. The seed group should be sure it selects varieties of these living barriers that are acclimated to your region. Contact nurseries, landscapers, farmers, or Cooperative Extension agents to see what varieties are commonly used in your area. Also, ask around to see which types appeal to everyone.

Because a windbreak necessarily involves a group decision, selection should be based not only on effectiveness but also on what is affordable. Everyone should also realize that living barriers take time to grow. Groups that can't wait might choose to erect fences and other lifeless obstacles. Woven fences that are about 80 percent solid prove most effective, because they baffle the wind without totally resisting it.

According to the USDA, trees will obstruct winds for ten to thirty times their height on the downwind side and from five to ten times their height on the windward side. Another consideration, if the wind blows steadily from the south side, is that care must be taken not to make windbreaks so tall that they block sunlight on the plots nearest the barrier.

Water Main

In the Midwest and other areas where people expect rain throughout the growing season, gardens have been established without water hookups. However, no area, including the Midwest, can rely on nature to consistently provide the average one inch of water per week that most vegetables need in the warmth of summer. Garden water is especially a major problem in arid areas west of the Mississippi River and likewise in the East during the midsummer drought.

Any vacant lot that once supported a residential or other structure (laundry, restaurant, school) supplied with water may still have a water main or at least a hookup to the municipal water system. To assure that plants get enough moisture to make the whole effort worthwhile, the garden should be tapped into the system. Any seed group with enough civic clout should be able to develop a complete irrigation plan with the assistance of an appropriate local agency or organization.

Some groups have been very successful doing this. During the middle of a drought in California, Richmond gardeners provided the labor to install an irrigation system while the city provided the materials and assistance through the Richmond City Council and Public Works Department. In San Jose, the Parks and Recreation Department used capital improvement funds to install irrigation systems (permanent piping and fittings), along with subsoiling and grading new garden areas.

Water should be metered at the site. This is so when the fluid is flowing, the garden person will be able to account for its use.

Laying Out Plots

After determining potential gardeners' apparent needs for space, the seed bunch must decide how to apportion the planting areas. When the group finally settles on a spot, this decision will almost always involve a delicate compromise between availability and demand. Plot allocations must be made fairly, and a line may need to be established where the garden ends and the waiting list begins. When the final allocation is made, the measuring, staking, and marking off of plots should be a simple matter of math.

If the garden is meant to serve as a demonstration site, pathways should be carefully considered during the planning stage. Pathways meant to accommodate tours and handicapped people should be wide enough to handle the traffic.

Some groups use rope, wood, or nothing but onions to delineate plots. Gardeners can also provide their own territorial boundaries, as is done in Boston's Fenway Garden, which began as a victory garden. In Fenway's case, it

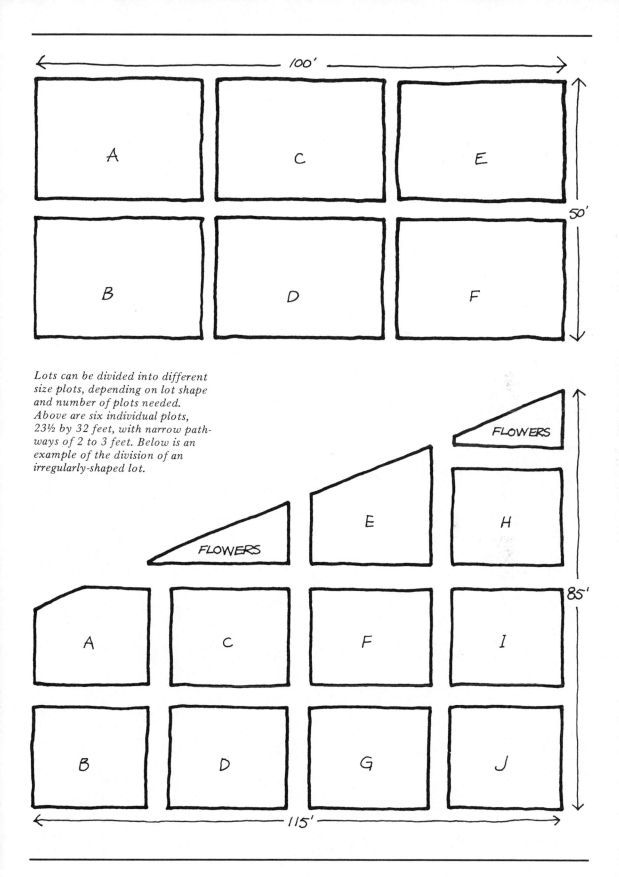

Lots can be divided into different size plots, depending on lot shape and number of plots needed. Above are six individual plots, 23½ by 32 feet, with narrow pathways of 2 to 3 feet. Below is an example of the division of an irregularly-shaped lot.

looks good due to the crazy variety of planted and inanimate borders. Anything works, as long as the division between pathway and plot is clear so that no one goes lumbering over a carefully tended planting.

Plots of a variety of sizes are offered by most garden groups, especially if the gardeners include not only large families but also single people. Allotted spaces don't need to be square or rectangular, but for convenience most gardens are divided into squares. A common size is 20 by 20 feet, but plots can be smaller if someone is not concerned with feeding lots of people.

Studies at Brigham Young University indicate that plenty of food can be grown on a mere 5- by 5-foot plot, even in Utah's short alpine valley growing season. In a test plot of those dimensions, fifty one and a half pounds of produce were grown in one brief season. Peas, kohlrabi, lettuce, radishes, beets, chard, and tomatoes were

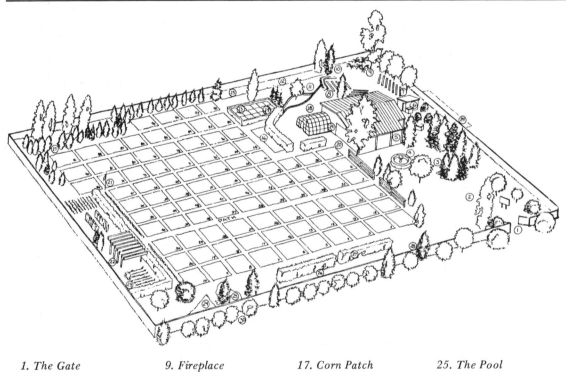

1. The Gate	9. Fireplace	17. Corn Patch	25. The Pool
2. Front Lawn	10. Woodland Garden	18. Rock Garden	26. Herbaceous Border
3. Pergola	11. West Terrace	19. Green House	27. The Green Wall
4. Herb Garden	12. Rose Garden	20. The Patio	28. Drinking Fountain
5. Garden House	13. Cold Frame	21. Flag Pole	29. Compost Pile
6. Tool Bin	14. Cucumber Patch	22. The Work Spot	30. Shrub Border
7. Tomato Shack	15. Rhubarb Bed	23. Fruit Garden	
8. Council Ring	16. Potato Hill	24. Chrysanthemums	

An ideal community gardens plan and layout produced by the Hilltop Youth Gardens, Bloomington, Indiana, a gardening project for children established in 1948.

grown at Brigham Young. Obviously, statistics on yields will vary greatly, depending on the type of vegetables and the varieties selected.

Few community garden projects offer plots larger than 50 by 50 feet. This doesn't mean your group can't have larger planting areas. Big plots have the advantage of allowing lots of room for corn and other plants that need to be grown in big blocks for the best pollination.

When the plots are first laid out on paper, the size of pathways should be figured into the plan, especially if wheelchairs are to pass easily. Also account for unplanted areas where children and grownups can relax together.

Segregated Sprayers

In many neighborhoods, the most important decision the seed bunch makes at the planning stage involves chemicals and their use in the garden. Great difficulties are bound to arise if the group doesn't grapple with this question: Should persistent herbicides, fungicides, pesticides, and other potentially toxic chemicals be allowed in the garden? If so, should those who wish to use chemicals be segregated from those who don't?

If persistent chemicals are allowed, conflicts will undoubtedly erupt unless chemical gardeners are segregated by distance and wind barriers from those who refuse to use these products. It is absolutely unfair for those who want to grow food without dangerous chemicals to be given a spot next to a plot where someone is spraying or otherwise using these substances. Segregating the so-called organic gardeners from the petrochemical ones is the seed group's responsibility. If the group doesn't account for this division now, trouble may arise later.

Also, future nonchemical gardeners need to have a way of being certain that the soil they use has not been infested with chemicals during previous seasons. Therefore, the segregation must be established for the entire life of the garden.

Some garden projects, especially those in the West, prohibit the use of toxic chemicals that do not break down over time. Your group would be wise to consider this approach, expecially if kids are involved in the garden. The problem is not necessarily the chemicals but their application. Many gardeners who use them don't go

93

by the labelled instructions. They overuse the chemical, thinking that it will have a greater effect used in greater quantities. This has sometimes created an intolerable situation in which the chemicals cannot be handled by the environment, and they build up to dangerous levels.

The entire question of agricultural and horticultural chemicals is a microcosmic example of the bitter battle now being fought between those who wish to garden and farm using methods that have been carried down through the centuries and those who raise food according to new methods, sold to them by representatives of chemical companies.

Room for Kids

No garden that includes family people should exclude kids. Indeed, children should be considered one of the basic elements in planning a garden. They can contribute a great deal to the spirit of the place, and they should have the opportunity. After all, they have as much (or more) to gain from the experience as anyone else.

If the group of potential gardeners is small enough and the potential sites are big enough, the seed bunch could reserve spots for kids to garden — on their own terms, with no need or expectations of productivity. Allotted their own special plot, aside from family planting areas, children could experiment and grow whatever they wish.

The garden could also include open areas for kids who show no interest in gardening. If insurance considerations allow, play spaces could be established, so kids could amuse themselves while their parents garden.

In all cases, anyone with kids should consider them a major part of the garden's very reason for being. They should not be denied the healthy aspects of growth and seasonal regeneration that flow through any garden.

Common Ground

Pick any location, forest, field, desert, or garden. Patient observation will unfold vast communities of carefully intertwined life. Plants are but a part. Natural communities overlap into urban human habitats.

94

In terms of plants, a community can consist of various members from many families or of members mostly from one family, as in grasslands. It can also be just one type of plant, as on a farm. The healthiest communities are the most diverse. But for purposes of pollination, some cultivated food plants grow best in a community by themselves. Corn, melons, berries are examples of plants that require this kind of singular togetherness. Gardeners must learn to respect the needs of many types of plants for these communities. This is especially true for neighborhood gardeners with limited space.

Some gardeners may want to consider the example set at gardens in Ann Arbor, Philadelphia, Newark, Dayton, the San Francisco Bay region, and other places where corn, asparagus, and other such plants are grown in common plots. However these "grow and share" plots, as they're called in Ann Arbor, require special considera-

tions before they can provide enough for everyone and so prevent feelings of resentfulness. Each garden must work out its own method for determining a member's fair share and then make sure everyone gets it.

Besides corn, melons, berries, and asparagus, other plants grown in common plots include vine plants such as cucumbers, squash, pumpkins, and gourds. Also included are fruit and nut trees, along with other perennial plants that must be isolated from areas of annual tillage. So, too, are herbaceous borders of flowers for cutting and experimental areas for uncommon food plants.

Signing Up

There comes a time, usually in winter, when potential gardeners must commit themselves to planting in the spring. Another outreach effort must be conducted to inform people of the dates for signing up — and for paying fees, if they are to be charged. How formal or informal this process is depends on the seed group, the neighborhood, and especially the scope of the project.

Big groups — more than a couple of dozen gardeners — sometimes require that gardeners sign agreements of intent and be assigned membership cards or badges that must be carried by the gardener at the site. These forms and badges are usually handled by the contact person. Other large groups may also require signing insurance waivers or other forms, depending on the sponsoring agency.

A few of the larger allotment-style garden programs require badges and membership cards. These must be worn at the site, so gardeners can be identified easily. However, only large gardens need these cards. Your face should be enough identification at a small garden.

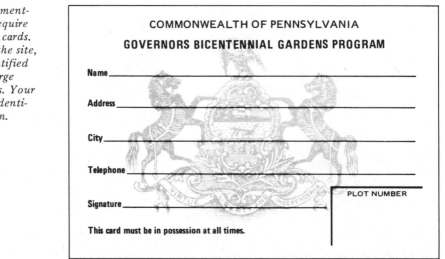

COMMONWEALTH OF PENNSYLVANIA
GOVERNORS BICENTENNIAL GARDENS PROGRAM

Name _____

Address _____

City _____

Telephone _____

Signature _____

PLOT NUMBER

This card must be in possession at all times.

Small vacant-lot projects don't need this much paper-work; someone's face and good word are usually all that's required. Gardeners are then registered only in the contact person's file box.

Waiting Lists

A waiting list will need to be started if the demand for plots is greater than the seed group's ability to provide for everyone who's interested. Most garden groups have waiting lists set up on a first come, first served basis.

The garden person must be watchful during the early weeks of spring to determine if a plot is being cared for or neglected. When it's clear that someone is not using the plot, the garden person will need to contact that person and politely ask "What's up?" The group should make it clear at the beginning that any plot will be revoked if someone isn't using and caring for it. A clear system of notification is necessary, so every gardener knows that after a third notice, the plot will be given to someone else.

Likewise, individual gardeners must adhere to the group's dominant attitudes about weeds. Most garden groups won't allow troublesome weeds to reseed themselves and cause more work for neighboring gardeners. Anyone who respects the food and soil-building value of many so-called weeds must live within guidelines set by the group. However, each of you should be allowed to determine what is indeed a weed in your own plot.

Revoking plots can be a delicate process, especially with people who are just beginning to garden and may be unsure of themselves. But it cannot be overlooked. Otherwise, the season will drag on beyond the point that someone can realistically take over an abandoned plot and produce anything worthwhile on it.

Will Weeds Invade?

Weeds were probably living on the vacant lot long before people decided to garden there. And if people can't keep their garden group together, weeds will undoubtedly reclaim the land. In this manner, weeds are both servant and master.

Some plants can also be considered "mother weeds." This is a name Joseph Cocannouer uses in his book

Of course not all weeds are friendly creatures that never cause trouble. Communities of a single weed, like crabgrass or bermuda grass or horse nettle, can be a threat to the garden and extremely difficult to get rid of, if left to grow un-checked. However, these weeds need never be considered such a problem that anyone in a com-munity garden should use harm-ful herbicides.

Here's what to do about trouble-some weeds. Spend a day with a real group effort concentrated on troublesome weeds. Be sure peo-ple know which weeds can be-come a bother. Identify weeds with bulletin board photos. See a county extension agent if you can't find photos yourself. Com-post weeds in active compost heaps that stay hot enough (160 degrees) to decompose them.

Weeds: Guardians of the Soil. Actually Cocannouer gets the term from a farmer who himself uses "mother weeds" to till and rebuild his soils.

"He considers these weeds as particularly good crop insurance," Cocannouer writes. "Furthermore this man has found that his mother weeds without exception are conservers of soil moisture rather than robbers."

This, written in 1950, directly contradicts the belief of most gardeners that weeds are no good because they steal not only moisture but also nutrients from other plants. Cocannouer has had a different experience. He lists amaranths, lamb's quarters, sunflowers, wild lettuce, purslane, milkweeds, ragweed, ground cherry, and others as mother weeds that will actually draw up useful min-erals and moisture from the subsoil, when these so-called weeds are selectively thinned to grow as companions among cultivated crops.

However, most gardeners are unaware of Cocannouer's writings and are unwilling to accept weeds as anything more than a nuisance. These people accept the popular image of weeds as damaging beasts, not unlike the giant frogs and flies that menace movie screens. This image is only an illusion.

Gardeners who understand the attitude of people like Cocannouer should be allowed to let mother weeds grow among their plants. However, there should be a point at which it becomes clear that weeds have exceeded the bounds of their nurturing role and have reached the point where their presence as a community threatens to overwhelm the less vigorous cultivated plants on nearby plots. This is when the garden person should require that the weed-infested plot be handled more carefully so the garden's delicate balance is not upset.

At no point, however, should herbicides be unwittingly spread around a community garden. They will destory the chances for other plants to grow there as well.

E Pluribus Unum

The fact that a city has one community garden project shouldn't exclude the possibility of others. Boston, New York, Louisville, Los Angeles, San Francisco, and Hart-ford, Connecticut, each have at least two major projects. In Philadelphia, Blaine Bonham helps run one of the most successful garden programs in the country. It's sponsored by the Pennsylvania Horticulture Society and serves over fifteen hundred gardeners on 130 separate sites. However, Philadelphians have lots of other choices. The county Cooperative Extension Service has a program generously funded by the EFNEP program of the USDA. The state Department of Agriculture has assisted gardeners through its Anti-Inflation Program. And many Philadelphians have been involved in the city's Block Garden Program that began in 1953.

Bonham understands the small and neighborly nature of gardens. He testified before a congressional subcommittee on gardening and told them: "Philadelphia is not very different from any other large city, and the inhabitants tend to remain in a small geographic area, creating their own quasi-political system. It is through this type of organization that an urban garden program would be most successful. The residents view a garden as an improvement to their neighborhood, working hard to farm the vacant lot on their block, but not traveling three or four blocks outside their neighborhood to garden."

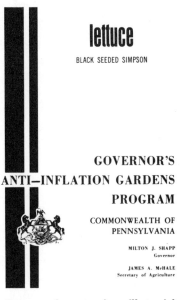

lettuce
BLACK SEEDED SIMPSON

GOVERNOR'S
ANTI—INFLATION GARDENS
PROGRAM
COMMONWEALTH OF
PENNSYLVANIA

MILTON J. SHAPP
Governor

JAMES A. McHALE
Secretary of Agriculture

Some seed companies will specially package seeds for garden programs. These packs were printed for the Pennsylvania State Program.

4
PLANTS

The Staff of Life

WEEDS GROW in any garden. Getting rid of them forever is impossible. But people still try, often using chemicals that are expensive and environmentally unsound. Common sense should dictate. Gardeners, especially those growing food, should get to know weeds rather than trying to kill them with questionable chemicals that threaten other life forms in soil, as well as threatening the health of plants and people too.

All plants now eaten by people and animals originated from wild plants. Weeds should never have to become a problem among gardeners. Many weeds are useful as food and drink. Some weeds provide valuable vitamins and minerals. Others are important additions to salads as well as working compost heaps. You'll find weeds easier to control when you learn which ones are edible and how they can be eaten. In fact, they'll probably cease to be "weeds."

Nestled among Illinois grasses (above) is a familiar plant. Few know its name and that it's edible.

Its name is broad-leafed plantain (Plantago major); it grows everywhere. The young green leaves of plantain are delicious when chopped up fine into salads or used whole as a steamed green. Older leaves can also be dried for teas. Indians ground meal from the seeds.

Plantain has been put to healing uses too. Chaucer said plantain could heal wounds and burns, as well as helping to relieve stings and itches. Another kind of plantain, narrow-leafed plantain, is considered a more tender pot-herb by many wild-food eaters.

A common weed found in cultivated areas throughout the United States, purslane (*Portulaca oleracea,* below) is a succlent treat. It can be eaten raw in salads and can be pickled, cooked, or frozen. The leaves and stems are edible, but the plants should be picked before they start to flower. The flowers are very tiny and found at the junction of the leaves and stems.

Purslane tastes best in the spring and fall, when it is full of moisture. Careful weeding around your plot and other's, so that the purslane isn't uprooted, may produce a potful of purslane a month after everyone has planted their plots.

Amaranth (*Amaranthus* genus, above) belongs to an old and important family of plants that includes many useful varieties. Some are easily used as leafy greens. Many varieties also provide a highly nutritious and productive grain.

Amaranth is the only plant outside the Gramineae family — all grains — that also is classified as a grain. Amaranths grow wild all over the United States, and they are known by several common names. In some places, especially the Midwest, they're called pigweed, but they are also labeled wild beet, red root, prince's feather, red cockscomb, tumbleweed, and love-lies-bleeding. Amaranth was a major plant used by Central American Indians.

If picked before they flower, the young shoots have a delicate flavor when lightly steamed. They can also be stir fried. *Organic Gardening* magazine has an extensive amaranth experiment going which involves 13,500 home-garden researchers.

Milkweed (*Asclepias syriaca*, below) is a hardy perennial that gets its common name from the fact that a white milky juice seeps from the plant when the stem is broken. It's also sometimes called silkweed, because the seeds are held inside silky tufts. Wildfood gatherers can prepare milkweed many ways.

In spring, the young sprouts can be cooked like asparagus, if they are picked before they exceed eight inches. Young leaves can be steamed or boiled for greens. Firm young pods can be boiled, and some consider the flowers a delicacy.

However, in all preparations of milkweed, boiling and pouring off the water is called for, until the bitterness of the sap is removed.

Dandelions will grow anywhere! A member of the Compositae family, dandelion (*Taraxacum officinale*) is related to lettuce, sunflower, marigold, zinnia, and chicory. Being perennials, dandelions often show the first flowers of spring and the last flowers of fall.

People eat dandelion roots, rootcrowns, leaves, and flower buds. The roots are scraped, sliced, and boiled in salted water. Crowns, leaves,

and buds are also boiled. The water should be changed at least once to remove the bitterness. Young greens can be chopped finely for salads.

Early settlers and frontier folk considered the dandelion a general remedy and healthful tonic. And have you ever had the pleasure of tasting dandelion wine?

Black nightshade (*Solanum nigrum*) belongs to that notorious family of poisonous, peppery, and otherwise dynamic plants, the nightshade family. Datura and bitter nightshade belong to the same clan that includes many familiar garden plants — tomatoes, potatoes, eggplant, tobacco, petunia, salpiglossis.

The immature berries of black nightshade are poisonous, but only when green and very bitter. Wait until the berries turn deep purple or, better still, until the whole plant dies and dries out. The berries will then become edible and provide the prime ingredients in many unique sweet-and-sour dessert treats, including pies, tarts, turnovers, and preserves. Some folks even develop a taste for them in salads.

Black nightshade can become a voracious weed that reseeds itself annually. It is also deep rooting and reputed to be a soil improver.

Plants Have Roots

ALL PLANTS HAVE ANCESTORS. Rootstock, tuber, seed encase whole evolutionary histories. Deep familial roots of the distant past intermingle with functional botanical roots of the present. Each plant's lifetime lapses onto shores of uncharted seasons, stretching beyond the horizons of human comprehension.

All plants belong to immediate families that likewise exist within immediate communities — just like bees, bats, elephants, whales, sow bugs, people, and other naturally mobile things. Likewise, all beings belong to ever extending families that compose the entire planetary community of life. They live, grow, die, decay, and support other life forms in return. All is reborn in this manner. Any lucid understanding of gardening should begin with these very basic facts of life.

Families of Plants

Common garden plants will reveal their true life histories to anyone who listens for nature's quiet voices and to anyone who looks beyond everyday obstructions. A botanic education is not necessary. Observation is the only prerequisite.

Within a couple of seasons, anyone planting seeds begins to notice something telling. Certain seedlings bear strong resemblances to one another when their first leaves pop through the soil.

106

In most flowering plants, these initial leaves are known as cotyledons. Among grasses, lilies, and a few others, these are known as monocots. They are not the plant's first true leaves. Cotyledons are formed from both sides of a seed's vital innards. Monocotyledons spring out alone.

Looking at cotyledons, most people cannot distinguish between radishes, broccoli, and cauliflower — or between carrots, celery, and dill. A trained eye may notice subtle variations in the color or texture of a leaf or a stem. But at this early stage, very few clues reveal the plant's individual species identity. The same is true of many monocots. Many grasses at this initial stage are virtually indistinguishable.

Similar sized and shaped cotyledons indicate important links among plants. That is, they belong to the same family. Radishes, broccoli, and cauliflower are members of Cruciferae, the cabbage family. Carrots, celery, and dill belong to Umbelliferae, the parsley family. A plant's cotyledons, then, serve the same purpose as a coat-of-arms or Scottish plaids. They are a signal to the world outside.

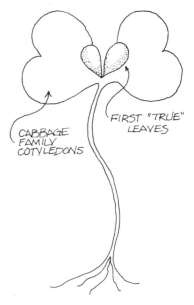

FIRST "TRUE" LEAVES

CABBAGE FAMILY COTYLEDONS

The Distinguished Families

However, the dividing lines among families of plants are not clearly etched. Some plants don't seem to fit the family mold. For example, tall sunflowers belong to Compositae, the daisy family, which also includes lettuce, endive, marigolds, zinnias, cosmos, and other less monstrous plants. Individual exceptions to family traits sprout along family margins. Nature and coincidence have allowed for crossbreeding among and within families, so it takes a few seasons as a gardener to recognize members of a family. That's okay; everyone has a lifetime to learn.

Other indicators, besides cotyledons, foretell a plant's lineage. The shape of flowers and the number of petals are leading indicators. Cabbage family members have flowers with four petals shaped like a crucifix, thus the name Cruciferae.

Leaves of plants in the same family are sometimes similar in shape, size, color, or texture. This is very noticeable in the parsley family. In fact, it's difficult to distinguish between carrots and Queen Anne's lace, unless you've planted the carrots yourself. Parsley and poison hemlock

TEN TOP FAMILIES

At least ten families of plants predominate in most gardens, including ornamental, vegetable, and herb gardens, as well as orchards and berry patches. These ten are commonly known as the cabbage, gourd, daisy, legume, nightshade, rose, lily, parsley, mint, and goosefoot families.

The only common garden vegetables missing from these are sweet corn, sweet potato, and okra. Most new types and varieties of plants are bred and selected from the ten most common families.

are similar enough in the early stages of growth to warrant any gardener's caution.

Sometimes a texture or aroma will help identify the family, such as the hairy leaves of comfrey, anchusa, borage, and other Boraginaceae members; or the distinctive aromatic presences of mint, cabbage, or gourd family relatives.

Sometimes a growth habit connects plants, as with many common bulbous members of Liliaceae, the lily family of monocots. This family includes onions, garlic, leeks, and others whose slender arching leaves stretch out from bulbs below the soil. Other examples are the vine plants in the legume or gourd families. Occasionally the shape of a plant's stem provides the clue, as with the squarish-stemmed plants in Labiatae, the mint family.

Throughout their family histories, common garden plants are united with the whole various world of plant life, including those plants called weeds, natives, or wildlings, as well as trees and microscopic plant forms. Choosing what to grow in a garden is an endless process. As you learn more each season, family relationships among plants will become clearer. Deciding what to grow each season will become simpler to comprehend as you develop an understanding of the distinct family relationships among all plants.

BOTTLE GOURD

THE GOURD FAMILY — *Cucurbitaceae*

Family link: Long vines with big fruits. Some sweet and some not. Some hard shells and some not.

Members: Cantaloupe or muskmelon, casaba, cranshaw, honeydew, and Persian melon. Also watermelon, cucumber, pumpkin, summer squash, Tahitian squash, winter squash.

Season: Long, hot summers.

When to plant: Early spring. Start seedlings in a warm window or cold frame.

Where to plant: Full sun. Will tolerate a bit of shade in the evenings.

THE GOOSEFOOT FAMILY — *Chenopodiaceae*

Family link: Compact clusters of small stemless flowers. Includes many useful herbs and plants long considered food by people.

Members: Beets, chard, New Zealand spinach, spinach. Also glasswort, kochia, lamb's quarters, orach, quinoa.

Seasons: Mostly cool, but varies.

When to plant: Spring and fall.

Where to plant: Beets need sun. Spinach and chard tolerate shade. Others plant themselves.

SPINACH

THE LILY FAMILY — *Liliaceae*

Family link: Many flowers are called lily, but only true lilies belong to this family. Petal parts are formed in triplicate. Seed pod forms deep inside flower. Leaf veins run parallel. Many members of this family grow from bulbs.

Members: Asparagus, chives, day lily, garlic, leeks, onion, shallot. Also, allium, aloe vera, fritillary, grape hyacinth, hyacinth, lilac, lily of the valley, poker plant, tulip, yucca.

Season: Mostly cool. Yucca and aloe tolerate heat.

When to plant: Fall or early spring.

Where to plant: All over garden. Mix with other plants. Mass bulbs together.

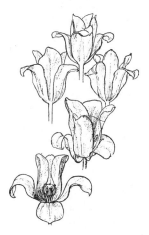

TULIP FLOWERS

CHIVES   ASPARAGUS   ALOE

THE DAISY FAMILY — *Compositae*

Family link: The most highly evolved flowers in nature. "Ray" flowers around the edge attract bees, bugs, people. "Disk" flowers in the center are for reproduction. One of biggest families, twelve thousand species, including many popular plants prominent in late summer and fall.

Members: Celtuce, chicory, endive, lettuce, globe artichoke, Jerusalem artichoke, sunflower, salsify, aster, black-eyed Susan, calendula, chrysanthemum, coreopsis, cornflower, cosmos, dahlia, marigold, painted daisy, Shasta daisy, strawflower, sweet sultan, zinnia, burdock, chamomile, dandelion, goldenrod, hawkweed, oxeye daisy, ragweed, sow thistle, tarragon, yarrow.

Season: Mostly summer. *When to plant:* Early spring.
Where to plant: Full sun for most. Lettuce, chicory, and celtuce like shade.

BURDOCK

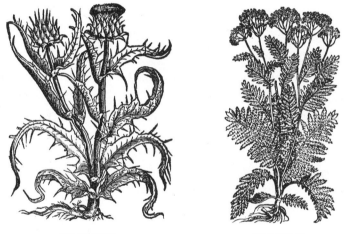

MARIGOLD   ARTICHOKE   YARROW

THE NIGHTSHADE FAMILY — *Solanaceae*

Family Link: Flowers are star-shaped with five points. Vital oils emit strong aromas in many species.
Members: Eggplant, pepper, potato, tomato, tomatillo, black nightshade, naranjilla, horse nettle, ground cherry. Also datura, salpiglossis, petunia, schizanthus, tobacco.
Season: Long, hot summers for most.
When to plant: Early spring, under glass.
Where to plant: Full sun.

EGGPLANT

THE MINT FAMILY — *Labiatae*

Family link: Smallish plants with square stems and sharp aromas. Leaves are found in pairs, opposite each other on the stem. Flowers are tiny and clustered together, yawning with two lips.

Members: Basil, betony, chia, catnip, henbit, ground ivy, hyssop, true lavender, lemon balm, peppermint, spearmint, rosemary, sage, summer savory, wild mint, yerba buena.

Season: Most members are perennials.

When to plant: Any time soil is warm.

Where to plant: Full sun for most.

FRENCH SAGE

THE LEGUME FAMILY — *Leguminosae*

Family link: Very vital family of soil improvers. Only plants that can transform atmospheric nitrogen into a form available in soil to plants. Intricate flowers look a little like butterflies. Seeds inside pods. More than seven thousand species of trees, vines, and herbs.

Members: Asparagus pea, bean, pea, peanut, alfalfa, clover, bluebonnet, lupines, kudzu, locoweed, mesquite, scotch broom, vetch, wisteria. Also acacia, carob, honey locust, leucaena, and tamarind trees.

Seasons: All. *When to plant:* Any time.

Where to plant: Most in full sun. Peas like cool spot.

TUFTED VETCH

CLOVER

BROOM

CAROB

WATER PARSNIP

THE PARSLEY FAMILY — *Umbelliferae*

Family link: Small flower clusters look a lot like umbrellas. Usually highly aromatic plants. Hollow stems and fernlike leaves. Family contains a few poison plants as well as common herbs.

Members: Carrot, celery, celeriac, dill, parsley, parsnip, anise, caraway, coriander, chervil, cumin, angelica, Scotch lovage, Queen Anne's lace, poison hemlock.

Season: Long.

When to plant: Any time, spring to fall.

Where to plant: Most will grow almost anywhere.

SAVORY CABBAGE

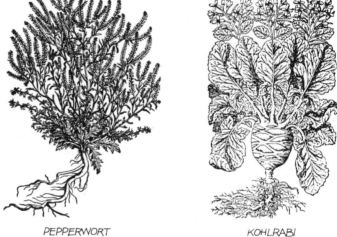

PEPPERWORT

KOHLRABI

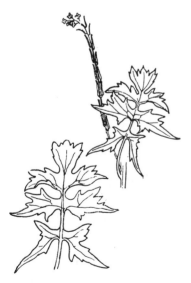

HORSE MUSTARD

THE CABBAGE FAMILY — *Cruciferae*

Family link: All flowers form the shape of a cross. Many peppery-tasting species.

Members: Broccoli, Brussels sprout, cabbage, cauliflower, collard, Chinese cabbage, kale, kohlrabi, horseradish, mustard, radish, roquette, rutabaga or Swedish turnip, lunaria, shepherd's-purse, stock, sweet alyssum, peppergrass, toothwort, watercress.

Season: Cool days. (Some gardeners say that Brussels sprouts are best tasting after a slight frost chills them on the stalk.)

When to plant: Early spring, late summer, early fall.

Where to plant: Shady spots if growing spring to summer. Sunny spots for fall-winter season.

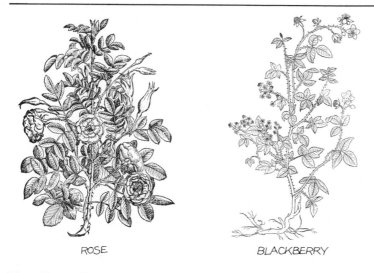

ROSE

BLACKBERRY

APPLE

THE ROSE FAMILY — *Rosaceae*

Family link: Stamens in a circle surrounded by curved petals, usually in sets of five. Most plants produce fruits containing seeds.

Members: Apricot, apple, blackberry, boysenberry, cherry, chokecherry, dewberry, hawthorn, quince, pear, pin cherry, plum, raspberry, serviceberry, strawberry, silverweed, rose.

Season: Most members are perennials, reborn each spring.

When to plant: Fall, but also spring.

Where to plant: Mostly sunny spots. Permanent locations. (Check around for the best local varieties.)

PLUM TREE

The Soil Shelter

ALL GARDENS ARE MADE or not made within the soil that supports them. If the soil cannot support life within it, it won't support much life upon it. This is what weeds — or their absence — tell you about a vacant lot that has suffered from compaction. Most soils in urban areas need some kind of help because they have been long removed from the processes that keep soils healthy — processes that are best observed on the floor of a forest, where decaying leaves and plant parts build up humus.

Humus is fine material of irregular size and shape that is decomposing and, thus, is giving life to microbes, earthworms, and plant roots in the soil. Humus is stuff that is dying, breaking down, and helping to create life from its death.

Good garden soils are composed of at least 10 percent humus. Minerals (primarily nitrogen, phosphorus, and potash) and trace elements (manganese, zinc, copper, iron, boron, and others) make up another 40 percent of good soils. The other 50 percent is empty space — room for air and water to circulate. And life, in the form of microorganisms, worms, roots, insects, is what holds it all together.

Sad Soils

Any good garden site needs soil that does not flood after a rain or dry out too quickly when the days warm up. Unfortunately, most soils on vacant lots aren't imme-

114

diately useful for gardens. However, soils have the capacity to heal themselves. They can be improved with time and care. Indeed, a major purpose many modern gardeners accomplish is to improve abused soils for those who will follow.

Soils need air to breathe. This capacity is especially important for vegetables and other cultivated plants. Compacted soil cannot breathe or allow water to percolate through it. Dense soil needs to be opened up. This is most necessary in urban areas where paved roads, parking lots, rooftops, and storm sewers prevent rain and other moisture from moving through the soil to the water table, where much of it belongs.

If soils on the vacant lots in your neighborhood are unattended and lifeless due to compaction and neglect, your group might be wise to consider raised planting beds. This will involve adding lots of compost, aged manure, and other soil improvers, but it will open up existing soil so air and worms can circulate and further improve the texture of the soil.

A Compost System

The key to a productive neighborhood garden is an efficient compost system, preferably one established at the garden site. Compost is self-made fertilizer. A heap of compost attempts to do in a hurry what nature does, in its own time, on a forest floor. That is, the heap creates humus from fallen and decaying parts of plants and animals.

Anything that is dying or starting to rot can be added to a compost heap. This includes old leaves, pulled weeds, unsold grocery produce, fresh manure, sewage sludge, kitchen garbage, and table scraps. But it's best not to use fat or meat in the heap because each attracts animals.

As long as air is free to circulate through it, a compost pile will "cook" from its own internal heat and, thus, will keep out rodents and flies. But in order for air to circulate freely, the pile must be tossed and turned by hand. Anyone who turns the pile should use a manure fork. Experienced composters estimate that turning a pile takes about five minutes. Doing this twice a week will produce one cubic yard of finished compost in three weeks with

MUNICIPAL LEAF MOLD

Many cities collect leaves from the trees on city streets, and citizens are responsible for gathering leaves from trees on their property and piling them up for the city to haul away. This becomes a big waste problem. Wasted is the energy and oil required to collect and transport the leaves. Furthermore, the leaves are wasted at the dump or, worse yet, wasted by burning and so turning them into air pollution. No one seems to realize that they're throwing away gold.

Leaf mold — decaying leaves — is one of the best soil improvers available. It's readily found in most neighborhoods. During autumn, members of the seed bunch should organize collecting crews to gather as many leaves as possible for addition to the garden's compost piles. Or they could go to the city dump and haul them back to the garden.

115

SELF-RELIANT COMPOST

No one could quite believe it. From only two markets, they collected five hundred pounds of food a week! Gil Friend and others from the Washington, D. C., Institute for Local Self-Reliance were impressed by the size of the load. But they still expected to prove "to ourselves and everybody else that we could compost in the area without rat and fly problems."

The area is Adams-Morgan, seventy blocks of low incomes and high expectations, in the heart of Washington, D. C. It was 1975, and the people at the Institute were ready to do anything to improve their deteriorating neighborhood.

But five hundred pounds of compostable stuff a week! "And we were just doing two stores," Friend said. "We were barely tapping the resources in the area. Without getting into household garbage, which requires separation and a change of habits, there were five other large supermarkets in the neighborhood plus maybe ten or twenty restaurants."

Using hand-carried cans, Volkswagens, and an occasional truck, the Self-Reliance compost crew transported the unsold food scraps from the markets to an alley behind a warehouse. There the scraps were contained in three 4- by 5-foot bins made of cinder block. Fallen leaves from other parts of Washington, D. C., were also imported to add dry weight to the mass.

"We decided not to ask the health department for permission," Friend said, "because we knew we would have been told no. We figured we'd just do it and then see how it works." It worked. And so did the crew.

just thirty minutes of effort. Because it is rotting, however, compost should be contained and covered, especially if it is situated in a city or suburban neighborhood.

Some gardeners add blood meal, phosphate rock, granite dust, and other soil amendments to the pile to assure a good balance of minerals within the heap. And, generally, the greater the variety of elements added to the pile, the more well-balanced the finished compost will turn out to be.

It's the responsibility of the garden person to make sure that gardeners understand the compost process, contribute compostable materials, and share in the tossing and piling. After the pile has cooked, the materials will turn into dark and sweet-smelling humus that can be added to the layer of topsoil, used as a mulch, or put into containers and used as an extra rich planting mix.

Many new gardeners need to be educated to see that compost is not a messy, smelly thing. The garden person should organize a compost demonstration to show that it's not at all mysterious. Perhaps the group could print a newsletter or flyer showing how to collect and manage a heap of compost.

Only once did the system experience rat problems. This was when rats dug under bags of leaves that had not yet been added to the piles. As soon as the leaves were composted, the rats forgot them. The piles were too hot for rats to bother, and they were kept covered so flies weren't a problem either. The compost was hot because the crew worked at turning it. Piles were turned with manure forks twice a week, as well as after every rain — at least in the beginning of the project.

"It needs tighter coordination than we had," Gil admitted. "If only one person is doing it, he or she gets really tired of turning all that compost."

Also there were occasional problems at the markets. "If the pick-up person wasn't right on schedule," he said, "we'd really hassle the people at the store. Because they'd be going to the trouble of having a special bin for us. And then the bin would be full and

nobody would be coming for it. They would have to do something with all the garbage that was accumulating and beginning to stink and getting to be a real health hazard for the store."

However, finished compost was used and appreciated throughout the neighborhood, including in the Institute's rooftop gardens.

At first the neighbors didn't think it would work. "They thought it's gonna stink," Friend said. "They thought it's garbage. You can't blame them. Their only experience is that it *is* garbage. If it's not handled right, it smells bad; it runs all over the ground and attracts nasty creatures. You have to just convince people, show them that it's not garbage."

Will such an extensive composting system work elsewhere? "Sure," Friend said, "if people are willing to make it happen. It's basically an engineering problem. It takes great coordination."

Manure Sources

Manure is important for the healthy growth of any garden. During their long histories, many cultivated plants have evolved to expect manure. Horse, cattle, rabbit, chicken, goat, turkey, and, in some places, human manures are used to grow food plants. People who think antiseptically don't understand the alchemical nature of compost, soils, plants — their combined ability to turn "wastes" into something of value.

Finding manure can be a problem in some areas, especially in places far removed from available sources of dung or in places where there is a big demand for the stuff. Stables, riding clubs, small farms, circuses, and even zoos produce manure in quantities suitable for gardening. Also sewage sludge (settled waste from treatment plants) is sometimes used if there are no local industries contributing dangerous levels of heavy metals to it.

Look around or call all the possible sources. Most people who have manure piled up want to get rid of it, unless they're gardeners themselves. Developing primary and alternative sources of manure may take some searching. It must also be transported to the compost sites, and this requires a truck, a commitment of human energy, and enough manure forks to move it. Gardeners must take care to use only aged or composted manure directly on topsoil. Fresh manures are too hot for young plants to use immediately.

How to Grow Good Soil

The best soils for gardens are half open space, where air and water can circulate freely, and plant roots can dig easily to find air and water. The first thing your group needs to do to assure that it will be gardening in good soil is to build up the soil's humus content, which will help lighten and open up the soil. The best way to accomplish this is to create a compost system. Most gardeners say there's never enough compost.

"The way you get a good soil," said Helga Olkowski of the Integral Urban House, "is to add organic material to the soil and let the animals, the microorganisms, do their work. They eat the organic material. The product of their activities — their excretions, their actual tunneling through the soil and excreting materials on the insides of those tunnels to hold them open, and the dying of plant roots — that's what creates good soil structure. You cannot duplicate this by physically going in there and throwing dirt around with some kind of metal implement."

Helga also points out that the organic materials must be kept near the top of the soil, where the oxygen is. "Don't treat soil as if it doesn't matter what's put on it," she continued. "It always matters. You don't want to compact the soil. You want it to be half air space, like the Taoist analogy of the cup. A cup is useful because it's mostly not there. The same with soil."

To Plow or Not

Many garden programs, especially in areas where farmers are amenable, have their sites plowed and harrowed annually. This not only requires a willing farmer but also the right timing. Soil cannot be too wet or too dry, and finding farmers at the right time can be difficult because they will need to plow their own fields first.

Plowing can also be expensive and unnecessary, if the garden site is too small to warrant the expense. However, if the site has over three hundred plots, or if most of the potential gardeners are seniors or children who don't have the know-how or energy to prepare soil themselves, plowing may be in order.

Gardens that include fruit trees, berries, and other perennial food plants, such as asparagus and artichokes, cannot be easily plowed unless these plants are isolated from the areas of annual cultivation.

A useful tool for small acreage is a Rototiller. Rototillers have the advantage of being able to shred plant materials and winter cover crops into the soil so that these materials compost there on the spot. Many tillers are heavily advertised and easy to find. However, they are expensive; a good one can cost four to five hundred dollars.

Small tractors, the size of ride-it-yourself lawnmowers, can also be rented or purchased for use in some areas. But again you must find someone who knows exactly when and how to plow the plots, and that's usually a farmer.

The main drawback to plowing and tilling with these machines is that they can work against the very thing they are trying to accomplish, which is opening up the soil. The weight of a tractor, plow, harrow, and even a large Rototiller and its operator compact the soil — especially hard clay soil — and reduces the ability of air and water to circulate through it.

If gardeners have the energy and ability, they might be wiser to use hand cultivation, including the use of compost and mulch, to prepare and improve the soil. This requires a bit of effort in the beginning. But over time, nature will take care of this soil-improving process. Microbes and earthworms in the soil will do most of the work that tractors, plows, and other machines are incapable of doing. These creatures deeply open up soils down to the layer of subsoils and build up humus as they go.

Dig It Yourself

Human labor and shovels are more compatible for small-scale horticulture, especially if the neighborhood garden site is smaller than an acre. Individual preparation of a plot creates an intimate connection between the gardener and the soil, and this also gives the gardener a stronger link with the whole process of gardening, which is as important as growing food.

There are various tools and methods that can be used for plot preparation. However, in all cases, gardeners should add humus-building compost or aged manure to the soil as they dig. Also, beginning gardeners should understand that topsoil must be kept on top, and digging should not be done if the soil is too wet or too dry. If the soil forms into a mudball when you squeeze a handful, it's too wet to dig. But if the soil crumbles as you squeeze, it's time to dig in.

Raised Planting Beds

Many gardeners on the West Coast and a few in the East have begun to employ an old planting technique used for many years in China, France, and other places where people wanted to grow more food in less space. The exact origin of the idea, called "intensive planting"

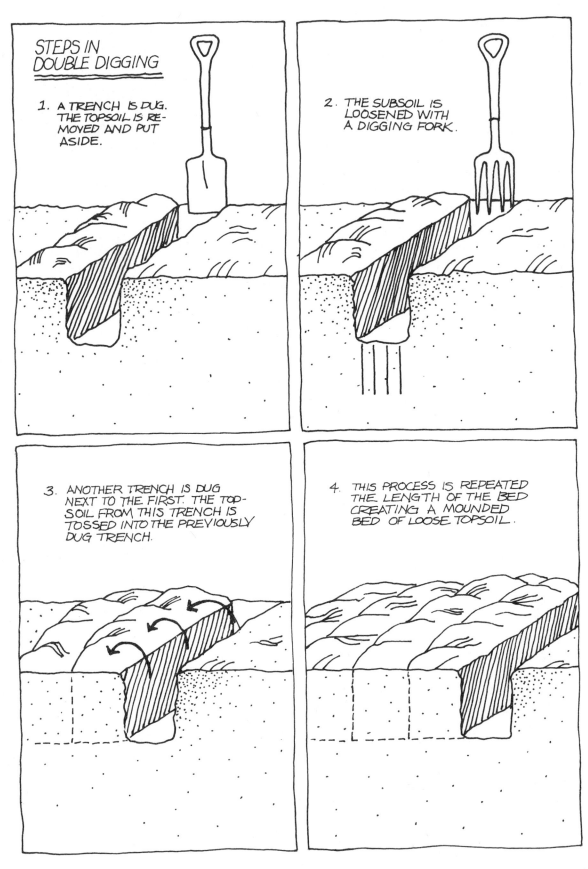

STEPS IN DOUBLE DIGGING

1. A TRENCH IS DUG. THE TOPSOIL IS RE-MOVED AND PUT ASIDE.

2. THE SUBSOIL IS LOOSENED WITH A DIGGING FORK.

3. ANOTHER TRENCH IS DUG NEXT TO THE FIRST. THE TOP-SOIL FROM THIS TRENCH IS TOSSED INTO THE PREVIOUSLY DUG TRENCH.

4. THIS PROCESS IS REPEATED THE LENGTH OF THE BED CREATING A MOUNDED BED OF LOOSE TOPSOIL.

or "raised beds," is unclear. But the concept works very well for vacant-lot gardeners because it maximizes planting space and keeps soil loose and porous. This is accomplished by "double digging" or "trenching" the soil to create raised planting beds, usually no wider than four feet and as long as the gardener wants.

The idea of the raised bed is to create rich, deep soil and to keep people from walking across and compacting the actual planting areas. People walk, instead, on a grid of unplanted paths around the bed.

Double digging or trenching involves digging the topsoil and the subsoil, in separate ways. The secret is to keep both layers separated while they are dug. Topsoil is usually dug with a flat-bottom spade. A trench as deep and wide as the spade is made for the width of the future bed (roughly four feet). This topsoil is put aside, and then the subsoil is loosened with a digging fork. The subsoil is not removed, only broken up. Then the digger moves on and makes another topsoil trench right next to the first. But this time the topsoil is tossed into the previously dug trench.

The subsoil in the second trench is loosened, then the digger moves on to the next trench. At each trench, the topsoil is tossed back into the previously dug trench.

This pattern of double digging top and bottom soils continues down the length of the bed. Then, after the subsoil is loosened in the last trench, the topsoil piled up from the first trench is tossed into the last. This creates a fluffy soil that is raised several inches above the level of the pathways around the bed.

To finish off the raised bed, a liberal dressing of compost and soil amendments is thoroughly blended into the topsoil, with a bow rake, to create a fine texture. No effort is made to create rows when the beds are planted. Instead, seeds are placed in "offset rows." The gardener completely disregards the "distance between rows" information on the back of seed packs. Seeds or transplants are placed as close together as possible. This limit is usually determined by the "distance between plants" listing on the seed pack.

Often two or three kinds of companion plants are mixed in offset rows according to their closest possible spacings. But this kind of interplanting requires experimentation until the gardener is accustomed to the distances that are compatible for all the plants involved.

Old newspapers and stones are used to mulch a garden in Louisville, Kentucky. The mulch keeps down weeds and helps to retain soil moisture. Many other materials can be used for mulching. Some folks even use rugs. Almost anything will work as long as it doesn't add poison to the soil or completely cut off the flow of air into and out of the earth.

121

Beyond Diggings

After a few seasons of conscientious soil improvement, a garden plot should develop that priceless commodity called *loam*. This is topsoil that is rich, healthy, and structurally sound. Gardeners who have developed this kind of soil need not worry about digging their plots annually. (If, indeed, they can hold onto the same plot season after season.) Nature does most of the labor for them.

What these gardeners do to maintain fertility is to lay down a thick layer of mulch each season, after the soil warms up. They do the same thing again after the first frost, when the soil is "put to bed" for the winter.

Mulch materials (straw, stable sweepings, leaf mold, lawn clippings, finished compost) blanket the soil with a layer of fresh humus. This blanket helps retain soil moisture and slowly breaks down into the ground during the season. The thicker this layer is — up to twelve inches — the better. Mulch prevents a crusty layer from forming across the topsoil and discourages the sprouting of unwanted weeds and volunteer plants. Thus the gardener does not need to toil so much.

Hoses left out are an open invitation to trouble. Some people leave them out even when hanging racks are provided. If individuals refuse to assume little responsibilities like these, someone else — usually a garden coordinator — must handle them.

Nothing Without Water

Plants are mostly fluids. These precious fluids are contained within the plants' very efficient and ornamental plumbing systems powered by the mysterious process of photosynthesis. Plant fluids function a lot like blood; they are a life-giving force. They can clot, seal up lacerations, and then go on flowing as if nothing had happened.

A plant's fluids compose and carry most of its weight and vital forces. These fluids would not exist without moisture in the soil, pumped through the roots to the utmost heights of the plant. Without water, plants would be nothing but dead.

Some community garden plots are developed without water, especially in the East and Midwest. These gardens must rely on rain or imported water. Sometimes, in mid-summer especially, this becomes a problem for gardeners who must then haul water in containers.

If the garden has an irrigation system, the garden person must account for its proper use. This may require daily monitoring to avoid wasteful habits, unless the group is small and extremely conscientious. In especially dry areas, or in times of drought, gardeners should be encouraged to put down a layer of mulch on their plots. Straw, newspapers, rocks, leaves, and all other kinds of other materials may be used to conserve soil moisture and cut down on the amounts of water plants need during hot spells.

Sometimes leaks are caused by other kinds of neglect. It may simply be a matter of a worn or missing washer. Replacing it takes a few pennies and a few seconds. But again, someone must assume that responsibility. Otherwise it won't get done.

Common Compost

WORKING COMPOST systems are a necessity in many community gardens. Compost systems don't have to be complicated, but they should be unobtrusive. Compost bins can be made of wood or cement block; they can also be nothing at all. However, compost must be covered with sawdust, soil, plastic, wood, or something. The pile should be turned after heavy rains or whenever necessary to keep it loose and warm. Compost heaps won't create bug or rodent problems if the heap is kept covered and cooking.

Compost ingredients (opposite, above) are temporarily piled at one end of the Wattles Park Garden in Los Angeles. Later the thinnings, trimmings, and prunings will be mixed with horse manure in bigger piles away from this site.

Compost can be carefully heaped without anything containing it. At Saratoga, California (below), compost is labeled with the date it was heaped and the ingredients put into the pile. In big gardens, heaped weeds can be

left to rot in place. At Sacramento's River Oaks (opposite, below), weeds have been cut and piled up right on the spot. This is a good way to handle future use areas or abandoned plots. The weeds mulch the area too.

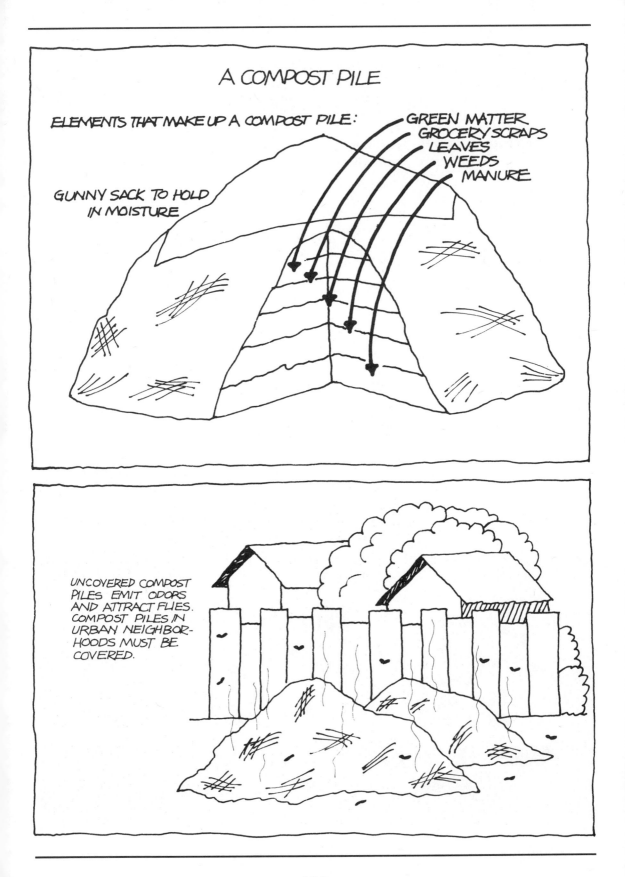

A COMPOST PILE

ELEMENTS THAT MAKE UP A COMPOST PILE:

GREEN MATTER
GROCERY SCRAPS
LEAVES
WEEDS
MANURE

GUNNY SACK TO HOLD
IN MOISTURE

UNCOVERED COMPOST PILES EMIT ODORS AND ATTRACT FLIES. COMPOST PILES IN URBAN NEIGHBORHOODS MUST BE COVERED.

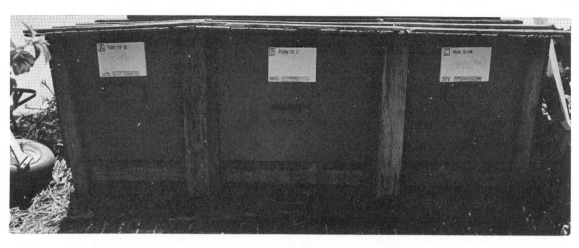

This three-box system (above) is covered, labeled, and out of the way. It has to be; it is located three miles from city center. The three open compost bins (below) are located in a more suburban setting at Ann Arbor's Ecology Center Garden.

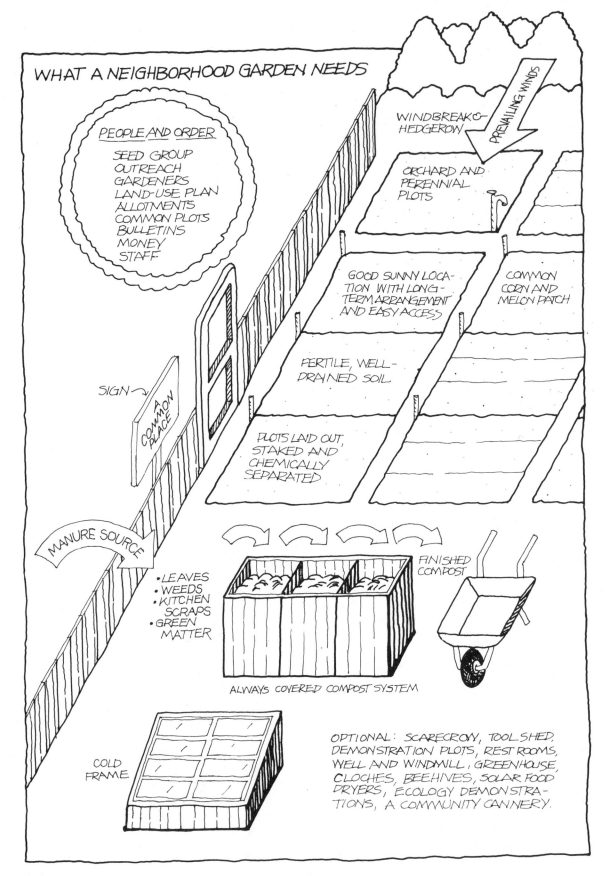

WHAT A NEIGHBORHOOD GARDEN NEEDS

PEOPLE AND ORDER

SEED GROUP
OUTREACH
GARDENERS
LAND-USE PLAN
ALLOTMENTS
COMMON PLOTS
BULLETINS
MONEY
STAFF

WINDBREAK & HEDGEROW

PREVAILING WINDS

ORCHARD AND PERENNIAL PLOTS

GOOD SUNNY LOCATION WITH LONG-TERM ARRANGEMENT AND EASY ACCESS

COMMON CORN AND MELON PATCH

FERTILE, WELL-DRAINED SOIL

SIGN

A COMMON PLACE

PLOTS LAID OUT, STAKED AND CHEMICALLY SEPARATED

MANURE SOURCE

• LEAVES
• WEEDS
• KITCHEN SCRAPS
• GREEN MATTER

FINISHED COMPOST

ALWAYS COVERED COMPOST SYSTEM

COLD FRAME

OPTIONAL: SCARECROW, TOOL SHED, DEMONSTRATION PLOTS, REST ROOMS, WELL AND WINDMILL, GREENHOUSE, CLOCHES, BEEHIVES, SOLAR FOOD DRYERS, ECOLOGY DEMONSTRATIONS, A COMMUNITY CANNERY.

An Unsung Harmony

EARLY IN THIS CENTURY, people who wrote about the environment told of the "law of togetherness," which also has been called the "law of natural harmony." This law attempts to describe, in general, the delicate balance among all living beings in a specific environment at a specific time. This natural law is now considered a major tenet of the modern science known as ecology. Togetherness and harmony are thus basic facts of life and are certainly fundamental to the growth of a community garden.

All families and forms of life are interrelated and interdependent, according to ecological understanding. A clear and present danger to any living form in a system must be interpreted as a potential threat to all, because it upsets the fragile balance.

Nature has built-in safeguards to prevent any one family or species of life from wholly dominating an environment. So it is that pests and diseases act as agents of health, attempting to restore diversity and balance. When various communities of plants, including random weed patches or established gardens, are destroyed and replaced by a monoculture, the health of the soil, and hence the health of all life, is potentially threatened. As long as monoculturing continues, all life forms suffer until pests and diseases restore diversity and harmony. Thus, health must always be seen as a community concern and not just as a matter for individuals to grapple with.

Chinese gardeners in Sacramento develop ingenious ways to coax plants to grow in two- and three-story stick structures. Small shade-loving plants, like lettuce and cabbage, are placed under climbing vine plants like luffa, wax gourds, bitter melon, beans.

Essentially Small Scale

Individual gardeners, who will be responsible for selecting what to grow in their plots, should realize that the world is full of choices, greatly exceeding the multitude of colorful displays in seed catalogs. However, anyone choosing plants for a specific garden plot should do so with foresight, especially those with small plots and those who want to garden primarily for reasons of health and nutrition.

After the size of the plot, the length of the growing season is the next major limitation. A family's appetite also plays a major role in this selection process. The capabilities of the specific seeds in hand, the health of the soil, and the disposition of the gardener will determine what grows there too. But the primary determiner is nature and its many active agents.

Choice Matters

Gardeners who face the challenge of choosing what to grow in a limited community garden space should not only pick plenty of the fast-maturing varieties of vegetables most favored by the family. They should also be careful not to let small sections of the plot stand vacant after something is harvested.

Selecting varieties with short growing seasons is a simple matter. The first thing most seed catalogs describe is the average time each variety takes to reach maturity. This is usually expressed as the "number of days to maturity." Country Gentleman corn takes ninety-two days from seed to maturity, while Early Sunglow corn needs only sixty-three days. The gardener who grows Early Sunglow will have corn — and room to plant again — almost a full month ahead of the gardener who grows Country Gentleman.

Although the specifics of soil, moisture, weather, and climate can affect these dates, you can be assured that fast-maturing varieties will be ready to eat sooner than late or midseason ones.

Additionally, many fast-growing soup and salad plants can be picked young and used before they reach maturity. Loose-leaf lettuces, carrots, beet greens, turnip greens, cress, swiss chard, mustard, green onions, and others may be harvested before they reach full size. As

130

always when harvesting anything, the exact time to pick it is a matter of personal judgment and need. But the rule of green thumbs is this: The young plant, picked just before it reaches maturity, is the freshest and best tasting. Plants that stay in the ground beyond their due date get progressively tougher and sometimes stringier.

Seed Orders

A seed is latent, intelligent energy waiting for the right time and place to express itself. A seed knows exactly what it has to do and exactly how to do it. (This is more than can be said for many people who have yet to determine their purpose on earth.)

Because they don't have space to waste, community gardeners must get good seeds from a reliable source in their region. Most major seed companies provide dependable seeds, although you should check the back of seed packs and read the date that they were packed. Out-of-date seeds may have been improperly stored and so have become worthless. For this reason, gardeners should never get seeds from discount stores or other nongarden suppliers. No one can trust seeds from someone whose main business isn't gardening.

Usually seeds should be used when they are fresh. Most seeds aren't viable after five years. However, a few seeds — especially those of melons and other gourd family members — are best when they're two or three years old.

A drying rack, normally used for clothes, has been put to another use in this San Francisco garden plot. The rack has become a structure for peas to climb upon. Any other free-standing device, especially those made of wood, can be used by vines for climbing. Old ladders, discarded wire fences, and other lattice-type materials may be scavenged for the same purpose.

Bulk Orders

Some neighborhood gardeners organize bulk seed orders to cut costs. The garden person and contact person should get together and compose a shopping list of seed varieties suited for your region. They can circulate the list among potential gardeners and set a deadline for orders. After the orders are returned, they shop through seed catalogs for the best bulk order buys.

Bulk ordering has two drawbacks. It may limit the choices a gardener has — but only if people seek no other supply of seeds; wise gardeners will get lots of seeds from many sources and bulk ordering takes plenty of time and effort on the part of those who do the organizing. But this is their choice, and they may enjoy bringing many seeds into the garden.

angelica	1
anise	2-3
balm	2-3
basil	1-2
beans	3
beets	4
broccoli	5
Brussels sprouts	5
cabbage	5
caraway	2
carrots	3
cauliflower	5
celery	5
celeriac	5
chard	4
chervil	3-4
collards	5
corn	1-2
coriander	4-5
cress	5
cucumbers	5
dill	2-3
endive	5
fennel	3-4
hyssop	1-2
kale	5
kohlrabi	5
leeks	1-2
lettuce	5
lovage	1
marjoram	2-3
melons	5
mustard	4
onions	1-5
parsley	5
parsnips	1-2
peanuts	2-3
peas	3
peppers	4
pumpkins	4
radishes	5
rutabaga	4
sage	2-3
soybeans	2-3
spinach	1-2
squash	5
summer savory	2
sunflower	2-3
thyme	2-3
tomatoes, hybrid	1-2
tomatoes, standard	4
turnips	5
watermelon	4-5

Seed Storage

Whether developing your own seed stock or storing unused seeds, the same requirements are involved. Unused seeds must be kept in a cool, dry place until it is the right time to plant them. Most seeds will last longer if you can keep them where the Fahrenheit temperature and relative humidity added together equal less than one hundred.

Dampness is the biggest problem in storing seeds, so all seeds should be sealed in airtight containers. Some gardeners use freezer tape to assure a tight seal. East of the Mississippi, and in other areas with high humidity, gardeners should take care not to store seeds on a humid day.

Planting Time

Any garden person must be well aware of your area's spring planting dates, and the garden soil should be ready for people to plant well in advance of that time. This is the single most important responsibility the garden person has. Too many people are relying on the site to be prepared, for one person to muff it. Also, the contact person must be aware of the garden's readiness and be set to inform gardeners, in advance, of the day that they can begin planting.

If individual gardeners are responsible for their own soil preparation, they must be able to work their plots as soon as the soil can be turned. After the site is staked out and ready for them, gardeners should have a week between site preparation days and planting time, so the soil will have a chance to rest and resettle before it's planted.

Transplanting Time

An early start is vital for many plants, especially tomatoes, eggplant, melons, peppers, and others that need a long growing season. These can be planted at home or in cold frames at the site, then transplanted into plots when nights have warmed to the point that nothing will be stunted by unexpected cold weather. Milk cartons, pots, trays, flats, or anything else that will hold at least two inches of good soil with adequate drainage can be used to give plants an early start.

Gardeners should plant more seeds than needed to account for seedlings that may die during transplanting. It's best to plant seedlings after direct sunlight has left the garden. This reduces the shock plants experience in the move. Also be sure the newly transplanted seedlings are adequately watered. If days are hot immediately after seedlings are put into the ground, provide protection from harsh direct sunlight by shading plants with mesh screens or boxes during the next three or four days.

In some cold and foggy places, small plants can be grown in cold frames throughout their full term. Plants like basil, beets, savory, and others can be grown this way to extend their seasons beyond the normal limits. Cold frames can be built easily if discarded windows and wood are available. However, glass covers should be designed so they can be removed easily during the heat of the day.

INSTANT COLD FRAME

Cold frames are great for starting plants early. What's the fastest way to make a cold frame? Someone in San Francisco's Clementina Garden had this bright idea: Find the nearest abandoned TV set. If it isn't already empty, remove everything inside. When you remove the picture tube, leave the viewing screen in. Be careful. If there is no screen, find clear polyurethane, glass, or fiber glass to tightly cover the hole.

Tilt the set to the point that the most sunlight comes through the screen. Open the bottom side or remove the set during warm days to ventilate the plants. But remember to close it tight at night.

Cloth mesh can be used on hot days to cut down the amount of harsh sun reaching young transplants. This also helps to reduce transplant shock.

Gardeners experimenting at the Community Environmental Council Educational Farm in Santa Barbara, California, discovered that this rotation of vegetables provided maximum yields:

Cleaners: potatoes, onions, leeks, garlic, and celery planted in raised beds topped with twenty pounds of compost per square yard of planting area. Followed by:

Root Crops: salsify, parsnips, carrots, beets along with approximately five pounds of compost per square yard. Followed by:

Legumes: vetch, peas, fava beans, bush beans, alfalfa along with fourteen pounds of compost and 1/4 pound of lime per square yard. Followed by:

Brassicas: kohlrabi, kale, cauliflower, cabbage, Brussels sprouts, broccoli along with fourteen pounds of compost and 1/2 pound of lime per square yard. Followed again by "Cleaners."

Planting Companions

Among gardeners, companion planting is a funny subject. Myths and ballyhoo abound. Lots of people talk about plants that are supposed to be "friends" and others that are said to be "foes." Long lists of friends and enemies are drawn up and strictly observed when believers plant their seeds.

Companion planting, however, isn't that simple. A good working understanding of the concept necessarily involves the agricultural principles of intercropping and succession planting. Generally, this means planting different things together that will mature around the same time (intercropping) and then, after those are harvested, planting still other plants as soon as the soil has been prepared for the new crops (succession planting). Gardens don't really have enough plants to be called "crops," but the same principles still work on a small scale as well as on a large one.

Companion planting and succession cropping doesn't really "chase away bugs," as some gardeners claim. In-

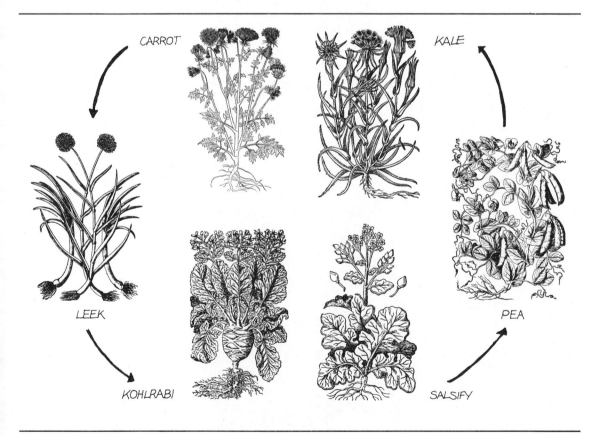

stead this kind of planting helps to create a vital and varied environment for neighboring plants along with other forms of life. Bugs will still be there but in different amounts and community arrangements, a mixed neighborhood.

Bugs in the System

Insects are the most maligned and misunderstood life form growing in any garden. Because of hard-sell promotions by petrochemical businesses, most gardeners have a completely distorted view of the purpose and place that bugs have in gardens. Rather than being pests that are injurious and harmful, insects (along with plant diseases) play a constructive role. They are representatives of health, vital forces at work in a natural system. They are signals to the gardener of an imbalance somewhere in the works. Usually this imbalance is found in the soil. But insects can also single out weak or misplaced varieties of plants. Seen from this view point, insects and diseases are like corrosion on the spark plugs of an automobile engine. They are saying that something else is wrong with the inner workings of the mechanism.

A diversity of bugs belongs in any garden, along with a diversity of plants. Indeed, when gardeners believe the sales pitch that a certain chemical will solve a bug problem, they are taking a giant leap toward perpetuating more problems all along the line of garden life.

Heavy advertising and dogmatic promotions have deluded many gardeners into thinking like monoculture farmers do. But farming and gardening are entirely different arts with entirely different problems. The best protection against bug problems in a garden is healthy, fertile soil and a diversity of life — plant, animal, *and* insect life.

Debunking Bugs

Although insects are an integral part of the garden, what if a hoard of insects is plaguing your garden and threatening to ruin your wholehearted efforts? What should you do then?

First you should be certain you have positively identified the insects causing the damage. To do that, you

SPECIFIC COMPANIONS

Companion planting *lore* is plentiful. As Chief Dan George would say: "Sometimes the magic works. Sometimes it doesn't." To learn which varieties of what vegetables grow well together, you must necessarily experiment and share information with other gardeners. Here are some combinations of plants that seem to get along well together:

Corn with pole beans growing up their stalks. This is an old Pueblo Indian method. Don't plant the beans until the corn is four inches high.

Corn with beets, turnips, onions, carrots, potatoes, purslane, or lettuce growing below.

Squash, cucumbers, pumpkins, melons, other vines with fast-growing lettuce, radishes, spinach, dill, cress, green onions, beets, or chard growing in the space that the vines will eventually fill.

Crocus, tulips, daffodils, other spring-flowering bulbs followed by zinnias, marigolds, cosmos, and other summer-flowering annuals.

Beans and summer savory, tomatoes and basil, peas and carrots, cabbage family with sage and thyme. All of these follow this rule of thumb: If they taste good together, they grow well together.

All-purpose border companions: Shasta daisy, borage, anchusa, garlic, aromatic herbs.

In this Kentucky garden, tomatoes are kept in check by planting them inside deep peck-size baskets. Notice how uncaged tomatoes engulf the area in the background.

must actually catch the bugs in the act. This often means waiting in the garden either late at night or early in the morning. All bugs must be presumed innocent until proved otherwise. If you can't positively identify an insect you've caught in the act of damaging plants, find someone who can.

When insect culprits are clearly identified, then what should you do? "You can't do just one thing," said Helga Olkowski, a pest-management specialist and co-author of the *City People's Book of Raising Food.* "That's what's wrong with pesticides. They're too simplistic. The system is complicated. You've got to use a series of strategies to deal with what is really a complex biological system."

Bug Strategies

When you're certain of the identity and damage done by a destructive bunch of bugs, here is a series of biological and common sense controls you can use:

Reduce the bugs' supply of food. Don't grow so much of what they are eating all in one place. If the damage is really bad, pull it out and grow something else — new varieties or other kinds of plants. Diversify.

Put out bait. If you notice cabbage butterflies going after a certain variety of cauliflower while leaving broccoli alone, use cauliflower as a "bait plant." Or if ants are hampering the pollination of corn and spreading aphids, put out small containers of honey under the plants.

Establish barriers. This includes things like tin-can collars around seedlings to keep out cut worms, nets over young plants to keep out birds, or rows of dry ashes around young peas to keep snails away.

Set up traps. Roll up newspapers and leave them out at night to trap earwigs. Then carefully remove the papers in the morning and discard them far from the garden.

Hand pick the bugs that are a bother. Go out at night or early in the morning and pick snails and slugs yourself. Cut off and destroy leaves infested with mealybugs or scale.

Increase natural controls. Import ladybugs, praying mantises, lacewings, assassin bugs, toads, purple martins, trichogramma wasps, and other natural predators to feed on bugs that cause trouble. Just be sure there's enough bugs for the predators to eat.

Be observant. Keep ahead of the bugs that you know can cause trouble. Destroy them before they have a chance to multiply, especially aphids, scale, or mealybugs.

Keep the garden clean. Earwigs, beetles, slugs, and sow bugs will multiply faster if they have places to hide. Remove boards, dead leaves, junk, and other hiding spots before bugs get a chance to settle and spread there.

None of these strategies will work all by itself. You must learn to do several of them at once. Keeping bug problems minimized will also involve communication among gardeners at the site. Identify potential and real bug problems on a bulletin board or by demonstration. Work together to promote sensible and uncostly solutions to your insect hassles. If the gardeners have a healthy attitude, the garden will stay healthy.

Bees are essential to any garden; they pollinate most of the flowering plants we eat. Beehives are kept in a few community gardens. Usually one or two people take responsibility for the hive, including the havesting and distribution of honey. If there are no zoning regulations prohibiting hives in your community, and someone wants to take the responsibility, beehives can be included in the overall plans for the garden.

Sink or Swim

Another attitude may help community gardeners control bugs and stretch the limited space of their plots. Although some will consider this heartless and cruel, others might liken it to the proverbial father who tosses his young ones, who stubbornly resist learning to swim, into the deep end of the pool.

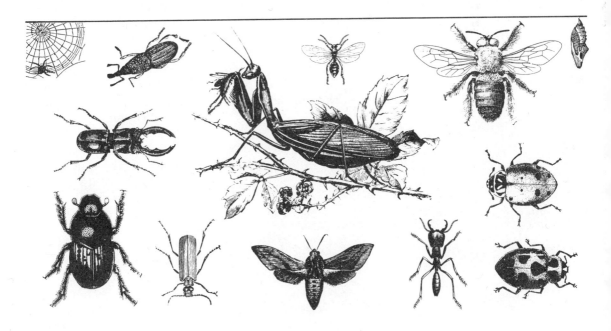

When you get around to planting the scarecrow, you'll know that most of the major effort in establishing the garden is completed. From then on, it's a matter of waiting, weeding, watching, pruning, and picking — the slow and easy part of gardening, the re-laxing part. Scarecrows do not scare most trespassers, least of all crows. But they do say as much about people's feelings for their garden as the sign out front.

Bottles of bleach can be cut and fashioned into revolving whirligigs that do more than twirl in the breeze. As they twirl, the plastic bottles rattle the pole which, in turn, vi-brates the ground. These vi-brations, according to some people, discourage moles and gophers from invading the area. Other gardeners use varieties of *Euphorbia*, com-monly called gopher plant or mole plant, for the same pur-pose. The root excretions from this milky family of plants are said to discourage burrowing animals.

Various screening materials can be scavenged and used to protect young seedlings from birds, cats, dogs, and big feet. Just be sure that the material is cleaned and isn't covered with harmful substances.

If, for some reason, a certain variety of something isn't growing well or becomes infested with bugs, the gardener would be wise to pull it out and plant something else entirely in its place. There are countless grillions of seeds to choose from on earth, and community gardeners can't really afford to waste precious time and space on weak varieties that may not really be suited for that spot.

This makes lots of sense, especially if the person's entire reason for being in the garden is to stay healthy by growing healthy food. Anyone with these intentions would be better off eating vigorous edible weeds rather than waiting for weak cultivated plants that must be nursed along. Slow and scrawny plants do not build healthy people anyway.

Face of Vandalism

According to the International City Management Association, vandalism in schools costs American taxpayers over five hundred million dollars a year. In suburbs and rural areas, vandalism against schools is worse than all other criminal assaults on private and public property. Vandalism in community gardens can't be measured by such monetary yardsticks. No one keeps statistics. Besides how can a monetary value be placed on blooming peonies? Garden vandalism can only be measured in the faces and words of those who have experienced such senseless acts.

Perhaps no other garden in America has been vandalized as much as the Fenway Garden of Boston. Of course, few community gardens have been around for as long either. Fenway, which began in 1942 as a victory garden, covers more than five acres and has room for more than three hundred gardeners. It is located in Boston's Back Bay region, a rough neighborhood. People who garden there know it. A couple of years ago, someone was murdered behind the wild reeds that border the garden. People don't like to talk about that much, but they still plant their plots every spring. Life goes on.

Frances Kingman has been gardening at Fenway for over twenty years. During the last three or four seasons, she says the vandalism has gotten a little worse. She remembers the time when Richard Parker, one of Fenway's founders, was knocked down by some thug who was ap-

Birds are attracted to gardens. Some, like purple martins, feed on troublesome flying bugs: flies, beetles, moths, and mosquitoes. Martins like to live in apartment-style birdhouses.

POACHER PSYCHOLOGY

One day a stranger wandered through the unfenced Richmond, California, garden while Jack Washington was tending one of his seven plots. Washington is retired and spends lots of time at the garden. After he determined that the stranger didn't have a plot there but was intently eyeing a row of untended cabbage, Washington approached the guy and started talking.

"I said, 'Say now, you see those houses over there, the one with the windows open? Some people are over there taking pictures. Some guy got shot out here the other night, trying to take something. They didn't put it in the paper you know; they wanted to keep it quiet.' "

The stranger backed off, but Washington kept it up. "I said, 'The police come around here all the time and take license numbers.' And I said, 'you walk across there some time and the police will come up. We got a certain password, and if you can't come up with the password, you're in big trouble.' I was sacking his mind.

"He said, 'I sure thank ya,' and I didn't see no more of him. Those cabbages are still over there too."

parently after his watch. She recalls a woman who was pelted by stones for no apparent reason as she tended her young seedlings one spring. Mrs. Kingman also remembers the morning she came to her plot at Fenway and found an unforgiveable mess; whole plants — chard, tomatoes, beans, peonies — had been pulled out and destroyed.

"I was in tears that morning," she recalled with anger. "It was cruel, pure viciousness. If they had taken all vegetables I might be able to understand. But peonies? They don't know how long I waited for those flowers."

Mrs. Kingman thought of relinquishing her plot, but she decided against it. She knows how much effort she's put into the soil over the twenty years. She knows how difficult it would be to get another plot, if she ever wanted one back. "What can you do?" she asked. "I just have to live with it, I guess. I never can grow enough of what everybody wants here anyway."

James Flowers, who has a plot not far from Mrs. Kingman, has come to accept vandalism as just another natural pest to be dealt with. He also has an explanation for why someone might uproot flowers. "They don't know what it is," he said. "They pull up a plant to examine it. If they see they can't eat it, they throw it back down."

No fence surrounds the Fenway Garden, mostly because no one really wants one; it wouldn't stop the vandals anyway. This is a quasi-public park, and a fence would be out of character. It wouldn't feel right, no matter how many vandals and thugs pass through. Besides, Fenway has survived many attempts to develop it into schools, hospitals, and parking lots. This garden has bloomed in Boston for four decades, and the gardeners believe it will survive the vandals too.

Alone Together

Most of the time, gardeners will be alone in the garden. Then and there, they will learn to appreciate the pleasure of silence growing around them. Anyone will be amazed at what plants can "tell" you about themselves and their needs, if you are merely quiet, observant, and removed from the distracting noises of the world around you.

Nature has many minds of its own.

On special occasions, gardeners may get together for group projects, as well as celebrations. Pick a weekend or special weekday well in advance, so no one has work obligations. Gardeners get together to haul manure, prepare soil, erect a fence, put in water systems, plant the first seeds, or any number of other special projects that will enhance the whole garden.

Not everyone will always participate. The ones who do will be convinced of the strength of their union, and their experience will bind them to the forces within the garden.

5
POSSIBILITIES

Some Can

COMMUNITY CANNING centers were very common in victory garden times. They have become more common again during recent years. Food price spirals and winter scarcities will spur further neighborhood efforts toward stocking up, as well as growing food. Gardeners in Indianapolis use the community cannery located in the basement of a community recreation hall to preserve food they can't eat fresh or give away. Use of the cannery is not restricted to food grown entirely in gardens. Fruits and vegetables purchased at the grocery store are canned here too.

Up to twenty people use the facilities at once, especially late in the summer. "It can get very crowded and very hectic," says Gladys Key, coordinator for the cannery.

Reverend and Mrs. Quentin Small prepare tomato juice and tomato preserves (below) for senior citizens at Crestwood South Housing Development in Southport.

Gregory Shirley (left), a staff assistant at the cannery, sets the atmospheric cooker for the proper time.

Each time equipment is used it must be thoroughly cleaned and inspected (below, left). If it isn't spotless, it must be cleaned again. No one can be lax about sanitation in a community cannery.

Mike Moran (below, right) logs in every jar canned today. Each jar is also written down in a record book. This is done to track down suspected botulism cases.

Reference charts (right) are clearly posted so that everyone will know the processing times, weights and equivalents for all the fruits and vegetables to be canned.

"Here, have some." Hettie Bingham (below) and Gladys Key hand you tomato juice ready for stocking up.

Further Growth

AFTER THE GARDEN SEASON ENDS, the seed group must organize a cleanup of the site and prepare for the next gardening season. This will necessarily involve building compost heaps and keeping in contact with present and future gardeners during the off season.

Some garden groups put together newsletters; others have workshops and tours of nearby garden sites in their area. At any rate, an exchange of ideas and information among gardeners near you can only benefit everyone involved. A regional listing of community garden projects and programs is contained in the appendix of this book to help make this easier for you. However, you should realize that many garden projects come and go. Some of the people listed may not be there anymore. If not, find out why their project dwindled or failed. This could help you keep your project alive.

eoa economic opportunity atlanta inc.

NEWSLETTER

VOL. 12, NO. 5   JUNE 19??

Drought Cuts Yield of Urban Gardens

More than $700,000 worth of produce for low income families is expected to be lost during the spring harvest, according to a recent survey by EOA's Community Gardening Program on its urban garden sites.

Expecting to have one of the most productive harvests since its inception in 1975, the gardening program now describes its spring crop as one of the worst ever, due to staff cutbacks and climatic conditions.

In March, the gardening program lost more than 90 per cent of its staff when Title X funds were cut. Forced to cut back its service delivery this year,

the program provided free seeds and supplies to only 3,500 families instead of the 6,967 families served last year.

Nearly half of these families report they have lost their gardens due to the drought experienced during May and June. Surveys indicate that the low income residents participating in the program have saved only $87 per family over the last three months compared to the $186 saved by families last year during the same period.

"Most of the problems have been caused by the drought," said Frank Jackson, director of the EOA gardening program.

"The lack of water killed many of the plants or rise stunted their growth causing a very small yield.

Since we work with only low income families, many of them could not water the gardens because of their already high water bills. It was like two variables working against each other," he explained.

The program hopes to regain some of its losses with its fall harvest. Jackson indicated that more residents than in the two previous years have recently been calling for seeds and supplies to start their fall gardens.

Residents of Grady Homes carefully tend their gardens in order to harvest as many vegetables as possible before the drought takes its toll on the crops. Left. Rosezenner Bearden and her son Christopher pour water sparingly on the thirsty plants. Right: Susie Mitchell picks stringbeans from her garden.

In newsletters, it's easier and cheaper to print drawings than photographs. But any picture looks better than none at all.

Winter Gardens

People in the South and on the West Coast will be able to continue gardening through the winter, if they plan and manage their project properly. For them, keeping in contact by means other than actually gardening will be unnecessary. However, not all gardeners will want to garden during the winter. The seed bunch should determine some way to divide the season into two parts, so those who want to have winter gardens will be able to do so. Just remember that these gardens must be started early enough in fall to be able to carry through the slow-growing months of winter.

Planting More Gardens

If your first garden was successful, and there are still plenty of vacant lots and vacant spaces in the neighborhood, and people in the group feel like expanding — you might consider starting another garden site or sites next season. Certainly this won't be as involved as starting the first one was, because you have already developed contacts throughout the neighborhood and community.

The seed group should, however, set realistic limits for itself. Sit down at the end of the season and seriously evaluate the effort it took to get the first garden started. Ask yourselves some hard questions. How far can you all go as volunteers? How much extra coordination will a new site involve? Are there any hidden dangers in expanding? Would everyone be spread too thin with new responsibilities? Or can you expect to find others who would do most of the work to coordinate the new site? All these questions will need solid answers that only the whole group can come up with together.

Others Needing Help

How about other seed groups in your neighborhood or community working to start their own gardens? Your group can provide information, local contacts, ideas, and other kinds of support that will help them take valid short cuts in solving problems similar to those your garden had during its initial seasons.

If anyone in your group has doubts about helping a new group, just ask that person to see it from the beginner's point of view. A new group may have attitudes about gardening or life that don't necessarily match up with yours. This should still not deter you from helping them. Whom do you know in the community that can help them?

Perhaps you can invite a new group to attend your off-season meetings or to tour your garden site. Certainly you will want to show it off. But don't just brag about it; tell

NEWSLETTERS

Some garden projects grow too big for word-of-mouth or bulletin-board messages. Newsletters and other large printing projects then become necessary. Your group must be sensitive enough to tell when a newsletter is necessary. Advice for starters:

Keep newsletters small and frequent, rather than big and sporadic.

Emphasize seasonal topics, upcoming events, and good ideas and advice from anyone in the garden.

Leave room for feedback, responses to previous issues.

Create special editions for special events, like parades or parties.

Use short sentences. Be direct.

Spell everyone's name right.

Have more than one person edit and copyread each edition.

Use pictures and simple layouts.

Put the headlines in larger type.

Study other newsletters for comparisons.

Find a printer you can work with.

149

Groups with nonprofit status
and mailing lists of over two
hundred names are eligible for
bulk mail privileges, which will
substantially reduce postal costs.
However, your group must be
approved by the local post office.

Postal Service Publication 13,
titled *Mailing Permits,* gives the
details of bulk rate requirements.
Call your post office and ask
them to send you a copy. Then,
when you're ready to apply,
see your postmaster or person
in charge of bulk mailings.

what specific problems you encountered during that first season and how you attempted to solve them. Also make sure your guests understand the problems you have yet to solve. In other words, give them the kind of help you wish you could have had when you were starting. Community gardens are especially worthwhile if they reach out to the larger community and so give back some of what they took from it.

Coevolving

Any seed group will evolve together, especially during the first few seasons. Some of the members may move on, but those truly attuned to the project will remain to continue the basic work of nurturing the garden through its seasonal chores.

The seed group should be ready to push on to new possibilities for projects extending beyond the garden. Perhaps someone can convince city hall to help you establish a community cannery or a greenhouse or a land trust, so your group can hold the land in long-term stewardship. If not, the seed group's reasons for getting together regularly may dwindle as the process of keeping the garden becomes more automatic as the seasons roll by. But this may be just how your group wants it.

"We started out in many cases with a high level of organization," said Mark Malony, a garden coordinator in Contra Costa County. "We had many people on the steering committee and a chairperson and regular meetings. Then as the gardens became stable, we let that ride. It just wasn't necessary anymore. The problems were working themselves out. People had learned how to deal with them, and meetings were taking place maybe twice a year."

Roots on
the Roof

NOT EVERY CITY AREA HAS ENOUGH vacant lots to support community gardens. What do you do if your neighborhood is like this? You may still be able to find room for gardens — if roofs are flat, easy to get onto, and strong enough to support the weight of people, soil, and plants. This was the case in the Adams-Morgan neighborhood of Washington, D. C.

During 1973-74, Gil Friend was driving a cab to support his self-directed study at the Institute for Local Self-Reliance, an environmental action group he and three friends began in the "club atmosphere" of their apartment building in Adams-Morgan. Friend was getting tired of driving cabs and wanted to spend full time working to improve the neighborhood, where almost forty thousand people — mostly poor — live in an area covering about a square mile.

"We thought of doing community gardens on vacant lots," Friend said. "But there were real limits to how far we could go. There were less than two acres of vacant land in the whole neighborhood. And not all of that got direct sunlight."

However, Friend and others at Self-Reliance realized that almost 160 of the nearly 640 acres of Adams-Morgan was sunny, vacant, and could possibly support gardens. That was the area covered by flat roofs. To see if gardening in the sky was feasible, they decided to experiment with a 4- by 8-foot planter box of tomatoes on the roof of their own building. The planter, which contained twenty plants, proved to be overwhelmingly successful. That 32-square-foot roof garden produced a crop of tomatoes equivalent to seventy tons per acre. On the ground, an acre of farmland would have produced only five to twenty tons, Friend said.

After that successful season, they decided to expand. Neighbors held several meetings at Self-Reliance. Finally someone said, "Why talk about it, let's just do it."

Up in the Air

Roof gardens began to spring up around the neighborhood, but many sank because the entire effort was very experimental. Wind, water, and intense summer heat proved that rooftops are unique and difficult garden environments indeed. However, Friend and others at Self-Reliance learned enough from their experience to help people elsewhere be more efficient about starting their own roof gardens. The Institute still maintains a demonstration greenhouse on its roof, and Self-Reliance members have gone on to other areas to start more gardens up in the air.

The Institute has outlined what anyone needs to start a garden on a flat roof. A stairway is important. If the garden is difficult to get to, people will be less inclined to tend it. Also raised walkways are needed to keep people off the roof surface. Planting boxes should likewise be set up off the surface, so they can drain well.

Because a roof environment is windier and hotter than the streets below, planter boxes dry out very quickly. Adequate wind breaks, midday-sun protection, and an available water supply are musts. The original Self-Reliance tomato planter was a foot and a half deep. "So it was a pretty sizable mass," Friend said. "But it was right up there in the full sun. We had to water it three times a day during the middle of summer!"

Before they painted the roof white to reflect heat around that planter, the tomatoes really suffered. "Anything that barely hung over the edge of the box," Friend said, "just cooked inside a couple of hours."

Greenhouses, cloches, and other plant shelters have proved to be the best environments for plants on roofs because the climate inside can be transformed into a more humid and temperate atmosphere. Wind damage can be stopped, sunlight can be filtered, and heat can be vented out of a glass or fiber glass enclosed structure.

Specific Load

Another major consideration is the "load specifics" of the roof. Friend says the way to find this out is to call the city engineer, building department, or anyone else responsible for enforcing building codes. But don't expect easy answers.

"We had a hard time," he said. "In D.C., they obviously did not know what the requirements were. We had to roll back through some old data to find out that roofs used to be built to hold thirty to forty pounds per square foot." Friend points out that load specifics will vary across the country, depending on the expected snow load. Generally, you can expect roofs in the South to be of lighter construction than those in the far North where roofs are probably much stronger.

In Washington, or elsewhere, thirty to forty pounds won't really support a big garden. "You can walk around on it or put a few containers out," Friend said, "but if you want to get into what we were thinking of as agriculture, rather than just a little bit of planting — using a significant amount of the roof space for growing — then stress gets to be real important. A cubic foot of waterlogged soil is going to run around eighty pounds. So if you've got two-thirds of your roof covered, loading eighty pounds per square foot, and it snows! You're really pushing it."

Gil Friend

Planting Medium

Due to the weight question, people at Self-Reliance experimented with several different kinds of planting mixes, including hydroponics (growing plants without soil). They found that vermiculite and perlite, two lightweight hydroponic mixes, weighed around twenty pounds waterlogged. However, these materials are expensive and energy intensive. They could not be easily recycled and had to be imported from outside the community. That's four strikes against them according to Self-Reliance standards. Hydroponic materials that made more sense in terms of local self-reliance concepts are too heavy when wet. These included sawdust, broken brick, broken glass, and flash cinders.

"A whole lot of our standards fell apart there," Friend said. "But we figured that at the start we would have to make these kinds of compromises to demonstrate the feasibility of the project. Later we could work out some of the bugs and look for alternative materials." Straight compost proved to be a good planting medium because it is light (if properly blended) and will hold water.

Another factor in the weight load was the size of the containers. This, too, necessarily involved trade offs. Small or shallow containers are best for lightweight roofs. But they also have less root space, dry out more quickly, and can't support large plants.

At any rate, people who plant on roofs should know where the beams and posts are located so they can put major containers at those points, which are the strongest areas on the roof. Pots and small containers can be judiciously placed elsewhere. Any container garden can be more difficult than a grounded garden, Friend points out, "because you're sacrificing the biological and physical buffering capability of the earth — the active soil layer, that whole mass, and the ground water. All of it. There's all kinds of invisible functions that you have to very consciously consider when you're doing any type of roof work. It's for sure an artificial system. But when you have no other choice, you have to live with it."

Beyond the Garden

GIL FRIEND OF THE INSTITUTE for Local Self-Reliance sees the ultimate value of community gardening as educational — not recreational or nutritional. He recalls a *Time* magazine cover during a beef boycott in the mid 1970s.

"It was one of their cartoon covers," he said, "with a fence in the middle. A cattleman was on one side with his cow, and the housewife was on the other side with her shopping cart. And they were both leaning over the fence, going 'Grrrrrrrrr' at each other. Now that kind of simplistic thinking has got to get blown apart, and community gardening is maybe one of the ways of doing it, so people in the city can at least understand a little bit about what farming is all about.

"And this may turn out to be the biggest value of urban agriculture. Because you know you're not going to feed New York out of New York. There's just absolutely no way, no need in even thinking about. You're not going to feed Berkeley in Berkeley for that matter. Or even come close. But what you can do is connect people up with the real world a little.

"So if they do get most of their food wrapped in plastic, they'll at least understand some of what went into getting it there — what it means to other people, what it means to society as a whole, in energy costs and social policy."

Exchanging Skills

But what can people do beyond their own small garden plots?

"The thing people can do is think about what's needed and then do an inventory of their community," Friend continued. "Trying to do it without any preconceptions about what you need, just what's there. A survey of space, of businesses, of skills. Door-to-door. What are your neighbor's hobbies? There's just gotta be situation after situation in cities where there's an old lady in a building with broken plumbing and the guy down the hall who just loves to do plumbing. But they've never met, and they've never even talked about it. Especially in the poorer neighborhoods, people have skills, enormous skills because they come from the land and from backgrounds of hard work. And more than likely they have the time. Getting this kind of directory compiled would be very valuable.

"We're not just talking about self-sufficiency. We're talking about interconnections — but an interconnectedness based on a maximum amount of self-reliance within your own locality, within being responsible for what you're able to be responsible for. Because this puts you in a much better position to cooperate and be interdependent."

Guerilla Gardens

America has more vacant and abused lands than it has people who are willing or able to cultivate them. But there is one good way to put this land to use and make it productive. The secret is to broadcast-sow vacant lots with seeds of mother weeds and hearty cultivated plants so their dynamic qualities and agressive root action can renew the land. Later these vacant lots could be used by neighborhood garden groups like yours or others. Or they can be left alone to grow and spread their wings as bona fide weed patches.

Robert Kourik is a guerilla gardener and member of a small group known as the DUMP HEAP (Diverse Unsung Miracle Plants for Healthy Evolution Among Peoples). He has compiled the accompanying list of guerilla plants

CAREFREE GUERILLA GARDEN SEED PACK

Seeds from any of these wild and cultivated plants can be used to start a guerilla garden. Simply break the soil a bit and then toss the seeds:

fava beans
vetch
clover
alfalfa
lupines
borage
black nightshade
ground cherry
cherry tomato
cayenne pepper
dandelion
sunflower
cosmos
wild lettuce
marigold
Shasta daisy
sow thistle
curly dock
sheep sorrel
shepherd's-purse
smartweed
milkweed
cocklebur
lamb's quarters
mustard
stinging nettle
goldenrod
burdock
nasturtium
amaranth
flax
rye
plantain

that can be used almost anywhere to restore abused lands without human effort or cultivation beyond the initial planting.

Seeds for these and other plants can be found in existing weed patches and by a selective search of seed supply houses. Kourik's group calls it the carefree guerilla garden seed pack. Wish them well!

Signs of Life

THE SPIRIT AND ESSENCE OF your garden is first communicated to people by the signs at the garden site. Notice how these signs seem to tell more than the name or sponsor of the garden. The design of the sign communicates the feeling people have for their garden. Which of the signs look most inviting to you?

A sign does not need fancy lettering or straight edges. The Project Rehab Garden, under Los Angeles power lines, has a loose hand-lettered sign (right).

In Harrisburg, Pennsylvania, the jigsawed edges and clear printing of this sign (below) can be clearly seen.

Some signs mix slogans with straightforward information about sponsors. But how much is too much for one sign? This sign (above, left) marks the Newburg Road Garden in suburban Louisville.

Two ways to say the same thing. "This is our food; please don't steal it!" The sign on the University of Michigan North Campus in Ann Arbor (left) appeals to students' scholarly conscientiousness.

Indianapolis doesn't beat around the bush (above, right). A spade is a spade, and a jail sentence is bad grammar in any language.

Mi Tierra means "My Land." Certainly these gardeners have strong feelings for their land. It shows in the sign (above). This garden in San Jose, California, is worked by over two hundred people, mostly Mexican-Americans.

Another sign (left) at the Mi Tierra Garden is stenciled on a board. It speaks for itself.

The sign for this Saratoga, California, garden (opposite) is carved in wood and blends well with its setting. These signs require lots of handwork, care, and time. But maybe there is someone in your garden who wants to do it.

6

SOURCES AND RESOURCES

Squash vines thrive in Boston's Fenway Garden.

Projects and Programs

WHAT FOLLOWS IS A REGIONAL LISTING of garden projects and programs in the United States. It is by no means a complete or firmly accurate list. A few of these folks may have moved on by the time you read about them. Such is the nature of the community garden effort. Many groups come and go, change names, combine with others.

However, the list will help you decide where to start in your area. Contacting groups near you — even groups that have failed with garden programs — could be very enlightening. The failures may help your group avoid the same mistakes or learn more quickly where to locate local allies and resources that you need for the garden.

These groups and agencies are often small, underfunded, and busy. Many are not staffed to handle lots of inquiries. Your group should always ask specific questions and respect the position of the people running the project. If you visit anyone on this list, show common courtesies. Make an appointment and keep it. Offer them information in return for what they provide to you.

The Northeast

Family Farm Project, Town Hall, Barrington, Rhode Island 02806. Phone 401 245-3103. Unique town program with three gardens surrounded by a farm, nature trails, and a cove. Administered through the town clerk's office. Leased allotments.

Fenway Garden Society, Back Bay Fens, Boston, Massachusetts. Large wonder garden in a tough old Back Bay neighborhood. Five acres of open wild space near Fenway Park, home of Boston's Red Sox. Loose organization of over three hundred gardeners, who have held onto this spot despite attempts to turn it into a hospital, school, and parking lot. It began in 1942!

Community Garden Project, Connecticut Department of Agriculture, Room 273, State Office Building, Hartford, Connecticut 06115. Phone 203 566-3552, Dave Nisley. Established by state law in 1975. Works with local sponsors. Uses all kinds of surplus state land — department of transportation, state schools, parks and forests, hospital, university, flood control, prison land.

Knox Parks Foundation, Elizabeth Park, 150 Walbridge, West Hartford, Connecticut 06119. Phone 203 232-7956, Mike Marchetti. Inner city allotments covering ten acres on school, church, apartment, and municipal land. Fees.

Gardens for All, Inc., The National Association for Gardening, P. O. Box 371, Shelburne, Vermont 05482. Phone 802 985-2565, John O. Davies, B. H. Thompson. Perhaps the grandparent of community garden organizations. Primarily funded by memberships. Working with many people and Gallup Poll to create a nationwide effort. Files on over twelve hundred community gardens. Free information package and publication list.

Adopt-a-Lot Program, Department of Parks and Recreation, 412 Spencer Road, Syracuse, New York 13204. Phone 315 473-4330, Pauline P. Norman. Cited by U.S. Conference of Mayors. One of the best coordinated city programs. No budget and no fees for gardeners. Park and recreation employees serve as staff. Began in 1974 as a volunteer effort —

many individuals, corporations, agencies, garden clubs. Helpful to others.

East 11th Street Movement, 519 East 11th Street, New York, New York 10009. Phone 212 982-1461, Linda Cohen, Gibby Edwards. Active group working to give people more control over housing, open space, and energy conservation on Lower East Side. Buys old buildings and helps people renovate them. Use of solar collectors and windmills. Big demonstration garden.

The Green Guerillas, c/o Council on the Environment, 51 Chambers Street, New York, New York 10007. Phone 212 566-0999, Liz Christy. Helps community groups acquire and use vacant lots for gardens. Also helps plan gardens and educate gardeners. Tool lending library. Sponsors "Greenmarkets" — a series of vacant-lot farmers' markets.

New York City Gardening Program, Cornell University Cooperative Extension, 11 Park Place, Suite 1016, New York, New York 10007. Phone 212 267-1460, Albert Harris. Received largest of initial EFNEP grants. Over seventy-five hundred people involved the first season!

Trust for Public Land, 11 Hill Street, Newark, New Jersey 07102. Phone 201 624-4015, Peter Stein. East Coast model for establishing land trusts. Small lot program with many families working small plots. No fees. One entire garden is given to perennials. Funded mostly by foundation grants.

Pennsylvania Horticultural Society, 325 Walnut Street, Philadelphia, Pennsylvania 19106. Phone 215 922-4801, Blaine Bonham, Jr. Big program with 130 lots, twenty-five dollar fee. Has big van ("The Gardenmobile") for major outreach. Mostly private lots or redevelopment land.

Urban Gardening Program, Penn State Extension Service, Broad and Grange Streets S.E., Philadelphia, Pennsylvania 19141. Phone 215 424-0650, Libby Goldstein, Coordinator. One of the pilot projects, funded by Congress in 1977 under EFNEP program of cooperative extension. Has four-sided program: community, backyard, 4-H, and container gardening. Newsletter.

Anti-Inflation Garden Program, Department of Agriculture, 2301 N. Cameron Street, Harrisburg, Pennsylvania 17110. Phone 717 787-5428, J. B. Reagan. Emphasis is changing here. Helped establish statewide program, including access to state land and seed distribution. Now local and regional committees order and distribute seeds. Good example of a state getting something started and then letting the locals take over and keep it moving.

The South

Economic Opportunity Atlanta, 75 Marietta Street N.E., Atlanta, Georgia 30303. Phone 404 532-7561, Frank Jackson, Director. Very active program aided by mayor's office. Free seed, fertilizer, some tilling, technical assistance to groups. Aimed at people of poverty level. Seven thousand families involved, including day-care kids, public schools, senior citizens. Plots to lease at one dollar a year. Cannery. Established as a result of a neighborhood task force about food.

YMCA Ecology Garden, 30 Woodfin, Asheville, North Carolina 28801. Phone 704 252-4726. Integrated garden, seniors and kids.

Garden Programs, c/o Agriculture Extension, Gainesville, Florida 32601. Contact for information about gardens in the north and central sections of the state.

Louisville Community Nutrition Center, Reitmeier Center, 1218 West Oak Street, Louisville, Kentucky 40210. Phone 502 636-3776, Jack Womack, Managing Director. Has five other projects besides inner urban garden. Private nonprofit corporation. Backyard gardens, public cannery, community farmers' market, free transportation to pick-your-own farms, and five food-buying coops.

Department of Human Relations, Jefferson County Courthouse, Louisville, Kentucky 40202. Phone 502 587-3631, Craig Panther, Garden Coordination. Took over program originated by a local bank. Three large allotments in suburban areas.

Parks Department, City Hall, Hampton, Virginia 23669. Contact Sam Reed about community gardens in the Hampton area.

Cooperative Extension Service, 15209 Marlborough Pike, Upper Marlborough, Maryland 20870. Ask about Greenbelt, Maryland, which is laid out for small farms and allotments.

Human Development Corporation, 1321 Clark, St. Louis, Missouri 63103. After Environmental Response left town, this program has dwindled from fifty small vacant lots to less than a couple dozen. Current agency may not be responsive.

Community Garden Program, County Extension Agent, 406 Caroline, Houston, Texas 77002. Phone 713 221-5020. One of the original EFNEP garden members. Did not respond to queries.

The Midwest

Project Grow, Box 645, Ann Arbor, Michigan 48107. Phone 313 994-0202, Ken Nicholls. For several years Ann Arbor has been a center for midwestern environmental concern. Project Grow developed out of an Ecology Center demonstration garden in 1971. Vigorous model for other cities. Over seventeen hundred gardeners on eleven sites, including a church, park, university, and apartments. At least one garden in every voting ward. So successful that city council names it as a line item in its annual budget.

Farm-a-Lot Project, City-County Building, 2 Woodward Avenue, Detroit, Michigan 48226. Phone 313 224-6330, Ann Bieser. Allotment program begun through mayor's office.

School Garden Program, Horticulture Department, Cleveland Public Schools, 1380 East Sixth Street, Cleveland, Ohio 44114. Phone 216 696-2929, Peter Wotowiec, Les Beamish. A unique concept that has worked for three quarters of a century in Cleveland. Students from third grade up learn about food while they grow it at school. The whole family benefits. This has become a model for other cities and towns.

Project Summer Sprout, Department of Community Development, 777 Rockwell, Cleveland, Ohio 44114. Phone 216 694-2046, Pat Jones. Young and active program. Attempting big goal: to establish a garden in every ward of Cleveland.

Adventure Gardens, Cooperative Extension Service, Ohio State University, 2120 Fyffe Road, Columbus, Ohio 43210. Contact Tom McNutt. Allotment gardens, fees. Autos allowed on site. Primarily a suburban program.

Benjamin Wegerzyn Garden Center, 1301 E. Siebenthaler Avenue, Dayton, Ohio 45414. Phone 513 277-6545, Ev Colhoun or Les Gamball. Maintains two huge sites within one public park. Over three thousand gardeners working twelve-hundred plots. Vying for Guinness World Record as "largest contiguous" community garden in country . . . still busy building a sound program. Garden project originated by City Beautiful Council, passed on to garden center.

Mayor's Garden and Canning Program, 6515 Delong Road, Indianapolis, Indiana 46254. Phone 317 634-5178, Harry Feldman. About three thousand people. Three large sites covering 138 acres total. Big plots, up to 50 by 50 feet. Fees. Initiated by mayor's office. Also aids backyard gardeners.

Garden Program, Public Housing Authority, City Hall, Chicago, Illinois 60602. Phone 312 744-3370. Models for apartment gardens. Started small, now covers whole city.

County Garden Program, Cooperative Extension Agent, Milwaukee, Wisconsin 53203. Contact Lee C. Hansen or Julian A. Wesley. Begun in 1971 in Milwaukee-Wauwatosa area. Includes telephone "Dial-a-Tip" service for gardeners. Did not respond to queries.

Garden and Canning Project, Center for Local Self Reliance, 3301 Chicago Ave., So. Minneapolis, Minnesota 55407. Phone 612 824-6663, Mary Goodell. Community garden, canning, tool library, skill exchange, and other economic development projects. Aim is to produce food locally for consumption in urban neighborhoods.

Energy Gardens, Parks and Recreation, City Hall, Winona, Minnesota 55987. Established in 1974 for less than one thousand dollars. Allotments on twenty-five-acre site. Maintained and administered by city. Fees.

Garden-A-Lot, Human Relations Commission, 701 N. 7th Street, Kansas City, Kansas 66101. Begun by an ad hoc committee of citizens, park and recreation, Model Cities, Youth Services Center, Neighborhood Improvement Program, Community Service Department, local newspaper, other agencies.

The West

Seattle P-Patch Program, 313½ First Avenue South, Seattle, Washington 98104. Phone 206 625-4695, Glenda Cassutt. One of the older garden programs on the West Coast. Over one thousand plots on about eight acres. Thirty-five hundred gardeners from ages one to eighty-three. Planting workshops, handouts, gardening aid, canning, freezing, and drying. Intensive and cover crop demonstration plots. Organic principles encouraged.

Garden Project, Blue Mountain Action Council, 19 East Poplar, Walla Walla, Washington 99362. Phone 509 529-4980. Small project in the eastern part of the state.

Garden Program, 6437 Southeast Division Street, Portland, Oregon 97206. Phone 503 248-4717, Leslie Pohl, Dan Sherrard. Program initiated by the Portland Park Bureau.

Eugene Community Gardens, Park and Recreation Department, 858 Pearl St., Eugene, Oregon 97401. Phone 503 687-5303, Lynn Mathews. Offers both year-round and seasonal sites. Year-round gardeners are responsible for their own soil preparation. Seasonal sites are tilled, sometimes by draft horses! Gardeners must sign an agreement not to use persistent chemicals.

Humboldt County Community Garden, Box 2576, McKinleyville, California 95521. Contact Simeon Murren. Serious and active group using earthworms and intensive cultivation methods.

Sacramento Community Gardens, UC Cooperative Extension, 4145 Branch Center Road, Sacramento, California 95827. Phone 916 366-2013, Lee E. Tecklenburg. Many city and county agencies cooperate in this energetic countywide program. Many cultures — Chinese, Japanese, Mexican-American, Vietnamese, black, white. Great model for small city programs.

Contra Costa County Cooperative Extension, 960 East Street, Pittsburgh, California 94565. Phone 415 439-4301, Mark Malony. Energetic countywide program.

Richmond Gardens Project, 1016 Nevin Street, Richmond, California 94801. Phone 415 236-0543, Cora Orr, Robert Hayes, Rev. Richard Dodson. Like Syracuse, New York, this program has no budget. Richmond runs on cooperation, sharing, and common sense. Directors look for public services. A parade each spring stirs up community interest.

Organic Farmers, 1820 Derby, Berkeley, California 94703. Phone 415 841-2683, Scott B. Funky activists trying to transform Berkeley flats into homes for chickens, ducks, rabbits, goats, fruits, vegetables, and other forms of urban wildlife.

Community Garden Project, 375 Laguna Honda Blvd., San Francisco, California 94131. Phone 415 566-1340, Roy Swanson, Susan O'Neill, John Forbes. One of the most diversified city programs. Many groups work together through a central greenhouse. Free plots. Centralized city compost system. Over fifty small lot gardens throughout town.

Parks and Recreation, 141 W. Mission, San Jose, California 95110. Phone 408 277-4661, John C. Dotter. Two developed sites, Mi Tierra and Mayfair. Four more in various stages. Sites in undeveloped park land. Innovative use of capital improvement funds. Will assist other parks and recreation people with inquiries. Informal gardening classes, more projected. Working on permanent gardens in parks. Also educational garden-farm-park near freeway interchange.

Rancho Vejar Farm, 37 Mountain Drive, Santa Barbara, California 93103. Phone 805 966-6016, John D. Smith. Innovative school program on private family farm. Kids tend pigs, goats, and other animals as well as compost, tools, and plants. Functions as part of Community Services Department of the county school system. Good model farm.

Community Environmental Council, 109 E. De La Guerra, Santa Barbara, California 93101. Phone 805 962-2210, Warren Price, John Evarts. A multifacultied group that establishes community gardens as well as recycling centers and the urban village — an agricultural and educational city farm.

Garden Program, County Department of Parks and Recreation, 155 W. Washington Blvd., Los Angeles, California 90015. Phone 213 749-6941, Seymour Greben, Director. For those outside the Los Angeles city limits who want to start or join community gardens. Leased plots for gardeners. More rules to follow than the Los Angeles city program.

Urban Garden Program, Los Angeles County Cooperative Extension, 1833 W. Eighth Street, Room 200, Los Angeles, California 90057. Phone 213 736-2445, Hedy Brehm. One of the initial EFNEP programs. Big bilingual program.

Neighborhood Gardens and Farms, Office of the Mayor, Room 100L, City Hall, Los Angeles, California 90012. Phone 213 485-6695, Mark Casady. Aiming to establish permanent, self-sustaining community gardens throughout the city. Run by the mayor's office. Helps neighborhood groups check availability of vacant land. Provides tractor, tillers, loads of manure. One city that has made it as easy as a phone call to start seeds sprouting.

Metro Farm, Inc., P. O. Box 1265, San Pedro, California 90033. No office. No paid staff. Private nonprofit community organization helps gardeners purchase, lease, or otherwise control the land they grow on. Provides insurance. Created out of Los Angeles's need to insure its garden program. All volunteer staff.

California Council for Community Gardening, Box 1715, Los Gatos, California 95030. The first statewide organization of its kind. Helps gardeners and organizers in the state to start and maintain gardens. Anyone working in California should contact the council for assistance and the names of current projects in your area.

Neighborhood Garden Project, Mayor's Office, City-County Building, Denver, Colorado 80202. Phone 303 575-2721, Jim Fowler. Turning a former government wheat field into gardens in the northeastern part of this city.

Plots clearly numbered at Sacramento's River Oaks garden.

Ways and Means

PEOPLE IN YOUR REGION may be studying and experimenting with many new ideas that pertain to community gardens, such as aquaculture, wind and solar energy, useful human energy, community development, collective living. Some are working to help gardens become a center for other kinds of culture besides horticulture and agriculture. Many groups assist people in finding land and funding for their projects. Most of these groups publish their findings.

Education

Farm and Wilderness Foundation, Brooksend, Plymouth, Vermont 05056. Kenneth B. Webb, Susan Webb. A series of special summer camps snug in the wondrous woods of Vermont. Ages nine to seventeen in camps that are self-governed "within limits." All but one of the camps have gardens. Camps are run according to Quaker principles. Nonprofit foundation. Send for brochures and enrollment information.

Natural Organic Farmers Association, RD 1, Box 1, Hardwick, Vermont 05843. Farmers, homesteaders, and gardeners. Agricultural self-sufficiency. Local and regional food co-ops. Newsletter, *The Natural Farmer.*

Scouting USA, National Office, North Brunswick, New Jersey 08902. Phone 201 249-6000, Thomas R. Dew, Special Projects Editor. Official headquarters for Explorers, Scouts, and Cub Scouts. According to the headquarters, scouts who help clean lots and prepare soil for community gardens can qualify for a merit badge. They can also qualify by recycling, scavenging, and gardening as long as the orientation is educational. Scouts are not a free labor source! See the phone book for local council office.

4-H Program, Cooperative Extension Service, USDA, Washington, D.C. 20250. Phone 202 447-6144. Local 4-H Clubs (ages nine to nineteen), often in conjunction with schools and cooperative extensions, have helped establish community gardens. Write Washington for the names of the nearest leaders.

Future Farmers of America, National Center, Box 15160, Alexandria, Virginia 22309. Phone 703 360-3600. Some local chapters have helped establish community gardens as part of their Building Our American Communities. Contact the local FFA chapter or the vocational agriculture department of your local high school or write the national office for the address.

Mountain Management Institute, Box 56, St. Paul, Virginia 24283. Workshops and seminar courses, great variety. "Co-ops: Powerful Tools for Socio/Economic Change" and "Community Gardens — A Way to Better Living." Fees.

Hilltop Garden, Department of Biology, Indiana University, Bloomington, Indiana 47401. Phone 812 337-6411 or 337-5007, Dr. Barbara Shalucha, Director. Founded in 1948 by one of three innovators of the Cleveland School Garden Program. Hilltop is a research laboratory providing "the nation with responsible and competent leadership for youth garden centers." Unique demonstration. Big greenhouse, pool, rose garden, orchard, woodland, herb garden, and potato hill. Cookouts.

Intermediate Technology, School of Chemical Engineering, Purdue University, West Lafayette, Indiana 47907, Ronald Barile. A student, faculty, and townspeople association interested in local community. Coop store, small-scale fertilizer plant. Cultivates federal funding for appropriate technology projects.

Living History Farms, Hickman Road, Des Moines, Iowa 50322. Phone 515 278-5286. Working farms from different eras — 1840 pioneer farm, 1900 horse farm, and modern farm. Agricultural museum, pottery shop, blacksmith, quilt house, and corral.

Men's Garden Club of America, 5560 Merle Hay Road, Des Moines, Iowa 50323. Phone 515 278-0295. Had nationwide youth garden program, but now only a few local chapters have kids gardening. Publishes *Gardener* magazine.

Farmers' Organic Group, 407 Furlong Road, Dusty Lane, Sebastopol, California 95472. Phone 707 823-0650, Sy Weisman, Nonprofit educational and marketing cooperative. Serves alternative food system and Sunshine Produce, a Santa Rosa collective.

D-Q University, Road 31, Davis, California 95616. Phone 916 758-0470. A freewheeling university for Mexican-Americans and Native Americans. A former Army communications base has been transformed. Students also grow their own food in university fields.

Food Advocates, 2288 Fulton Street, Berkeley, California 94704. Free posters and other information handouts on food stamps and nutrition. Community help. Newsletter.

Public Media Center, 2751 Hyde St., San Francisco, California 94109. Phone 415 885-0200. Helps people put together public service announcements and otherwise gain access to media. Newsletter.

Learning Resources Center, West Valley College, 14000 Fruitvale Ave., Saratoga, California 95070. Phone 408 867-2200, ex. 472. Video tapes of lectures given by Alan Chadwick at an urban garden symposium on campus. Also other garden resources available on audio tape, film, and other media.

National Garden Bureau, 4546 El Camino Real, Suite A, Los Altos, California 94022. Phone 415 941-2030, James W. Wilson, Executive Director. A nonprofit educational service of the North American vegetable and flower seed industry. Good source of all kinds of garden information. Make specific inquiry. Not directly involved in community gardens, but "standing on the sidelines and cheering."

Institute for Planning Education, School of Urban and Regional Planning, Bruce Hall 301, University of Southern California, Los Angeles, California 90007. Phone 213 741-2559, Emily Card. Sponsors a conference on urban agriculture. "The garden can be considered a component of an urban planning process that addresses such issues as the recycling of water and organic wastes, land-use planning."

Land

The Sam Ely Community Land Trust, 136 Maine St., Brunswick, Maine 04011. One of the oldest land trusts in the country. Sam Ely publishes the *Maine Land Advocate*. A good group to be in touch with. They're thoughtful and responsible in their promotion of trusts.

Community Land Trust Center, 639 Massachusetts Ave., Cambridge, Massachusetts 01439.

The Nature Conservancy, 1800 North Kent St., Arlington, Virginia 22209. Offices in many parts of the country. Has acquired numerous areas for public access. Emphasis on wilderness land.

The Evergreen Land Trust, P. O. Box 303, Clear Lake, Washington 98235. First land trust in the country to receive a federally nonprofit, tax exempt status. Looking at ways to expand the trust concept.

The People's Land Trust, 1000 Harris St., Bellingham, Washington 98225. Unique urban-centered trust. Helps on problems with urban properties held in perpetuity.

Northern California Land Trust, 330 Ellis St., Room 504, San Francisco, California 94102. Helps to provide farmable lands to otherwise disenfranchised people. Newsletter three dollars a year, membership six dollars.

People for Open Space, 46 Kearny St., San Francisco, California 94108. An active group working to establish open space and to stop sprawling developments in the San Francisco Bay Area.

The Trust for Public Land, 82 Second St., San Francisco, California 94105. Phone 415 495-4014, Mitch Hardin or Steve Costa. Oriented toward urban/suburban open space property. Various large corporations and landowners have given land to the public through them.

Funding

Arca Foundation, 100 East 85th St., New York, New York 10028. Phone 212 861-8300, Frank D. Dobyns. Small, private, nonprofit. Gives grants in the fields of population studies, population control, food and nutrition, and appropriate technology, particularly as it relates to small-scale farming. Concerned with stimulating local and community participation.

Foundation Center, 888 Seventh Ave., New York, New York 10019. Phone 212 489-8610. Or 1001 Connecticut Ave. N.W., Washington, D.C. 20036. Phone 202 331-1400. Disseminates information about philanthropic groups. Public reference library about foundations and their grant-giving interests. Over fifty regional offices. For free information start by contacting New York or Washington, D.C., office.

The Grantsmanship Center, 1728 "L" St. N.W., Suite 300, Washington, D.C. 20036. Phone 202 331-0833. Or 1015 West Olympic Blvd., Los Angeles, California 90015. Phone 213 485-9094. Works with nonprofit groups and public agencies in planning and resource development. Workshops. Magazine about government and nongovernment funds. In-house research staff and library.

Donors' Forum of Chicago, 208 S. LaSalle, Chicago, Illinois 60604. Information about philanthropic foundations. Public reference library about foundations and grants.

Alchemy

The New Alchemy Institute, Box 432, Woods Hole, Massachusetts 02543. Phone 617 563-2655, Earle Barnhart. Since 1969, has conducted experiments in aquaculture, renewable energy systems, coherent life systems. Hopes to develop food forests.

Information and Education Center, Organic Gardening and Farming Research Institute, c/o Organic Park, Emmaus, Pennsylvania 18049. Employees of Rodale Press have plots at the 305-acre experimental farm, for both personal and experimental gardening. Demonstration plots. Lots is always happening here.

Rural Advancement Fund, 2128 Commonwealth Ave., Charlotte, North Carolina 28205. Phone 704 334-3051, James M. Pierce. Frank Porter Graham Experimental Farm and Training Center. Free training on 650 acres to low-income people who want to learn to farm a small holding. Soil preparation, organic farming, marketing, rural related vocational skills, cooperative and community organizing.

The Farm, 156 Drakes Lane, Summertown, Tennessee 38483. Phone 615 964-3574. "A spiritual community owned and operated by the people." Eleven hundred people on over seventeen hundred acres of land. Twelve sister communities. They research and distribute vegetable protein. Farm and garden their own food and give tons away yearly to "anybody who needs it." Several books in print.

New Pioneer Cooperative Society, 529 S. Gilbert, Iowa City, Iowa 52240. Phone 319 338-5300. Natural foods coop managed by collective. They sell local organic produce, commercial natural foods, books. Newsletter.

Sundance Restaurant, 127 Harbor S.E., Albuquerque, New Mexico, 87106. Phone 505 255-0986, Bill Cooke, John Starino, Wendy Ostrow. Cooperative garden and solar greenhouse that partially feeds the customers. Corn, beans, squash, lettuce, tomatoes, sunflowers, mung and alfalfa sprouts. This restaurant might let you pick your salad.

Osha Food Cooperative and Collective Garden, Alameda, New Mexico 87114, Peter Stege. Around twenty people make a living on this collective garden farm and store. Many vegetables, including lots of peppers and chilis. Ten acres. Intense hand labor — mulch, mulch, mulch.

Ecotope-Pragtree, 747 16th East, Seattle, Washington 98112. Pragtree Farm has a solar greenhouse, and Ecotope has a passive-solar-heated aquaculture greenhouse near Seattle.

Round Valley Garden Project, Route 1, Box 98, Covelo, California 95428. Phone 707 983-4161, Raymond Chavez or Richard Joos. Apprentices study intensive horticulture at the most incredible group garden in America. Seven acres under thick cultivation. Serious evaluations of self and group growth. Lectures and outreach. Limited enrollment.

National Center for Appropriate Technology, Box 3838, Butte, Montana 59701. Phone 406 723-6533, James Schmidt. Has initial grant of three million dollars to provide technical assistance and small grant support to appropriate technology projects with direct relevance to low-income communities. Collects and gives out information by newsletter, quarterly, and hotline. Regional outreach organizers. Research and development.

Office of Appropriate Technology, P. O. Box 1677, Sacramento, California 95808. Phone 916 445-1803, Rosemary Meninger. Advocates change in the areas of job development, resource conservation, environmental protection, and community development. Seminars, demonstration projects, and publications. Write for programs and reports.

Integral Urban House, Farallones Institute, 1516 Fifth St., Berkeley, California 94710. Phone 415 525-1150, Helga and William Olkowski, Education and Research; Tom Javits, House Manager. Study and demonstration of environmentally sound strategies and techniques of homesite food production, community development, energy conservation and generation, waste recycling, and pest management suitable for application in urban areas. Open to the public. Demonstrations of solar collection, gray-water reclamation, waterless biological toilet, raising of high quality animal protein, intensive food gardening. Educational programs and publications. A guiding light.

Mutual Aid, Ecology Center, 2179 Allston Way, Berkeley, California 94704, Bob Fabian. Three-point urban program to study (1) community-based economic development, (2) energy conservation and alternative energy, (3) urban agriculture — research the limits of community self-sufficiency in food and optimum combinations of vacant-lot and backyard gardening, rooftop gardens, hydroponics, aquaculture, the leasing of nearby agricultural land, and coalitions with progressive rural farms. Hopes to provide demonstrations, booklets, and films.

Earthwork, 3410 19th St., San Francisco, California 94110. Phone 415 648-2094. Urban resource center for study of land and food. Films, slides, tape shows, educational display panels, books for sale. Library. Collective works on urban composting and earthworms. Studying effects of pollution on city-grown food.

Ecology Action of Midpeninsula, 2225 El Camino Real, Palo Alto, California 94306. Phone 415 328-6752. John Jeavons and Robin Leler. Research, documentation, education, and statistics about California intensive raised-bed garden methods. Demonstration project, nonprofit supply store, library, information center, newsletter. Will answer specific questions if you send self-addressed stamped envelope with two stamps. Send for publishing list. They have several reports.

Ecohouse, 65 Eckley Lane, Walnut Creek, California 94598. Phone 415 937-2072, Mark Malony. Environmental living center for Contra Costa County (northeast of San Francisco). An "integral suburban house" with not only community garden space but also orchard, bees, worm bins, and appropriate technology experiments. An active, demonstrative ecology center and information exchange. Publishes fine newsletter, *Down to Earth*.

Central Coast Counties Development Corporation, 7000 Soquel Drive, Aptos, California 95003. Phone 408 688-9000, Alfredo Navarro. Agriculture-based community economic development mostly for rural Mexican-Americans in three California counties. Helps people become farmers, landowners, home-owners, managers of their own enterprises. Has greenhouses, nutrition programs, job training, community services, other cooperative ventures.

Biodynamic Farming and Gardening Association, 17240 Los Alamos St., Granada Hills, California 91344. Phone 213 363-1893. Good resource for intensive gardens. Has biodynamic mixes, literature, conferences. "Fore-runner Farm Project," a three month course on biodynamics and Rudolf Steiner.

Sunburst Communities, 808 East Cota St., Santa Barbara, California 93103. Religiously oriented, self-sustaining community of store-keepers, shepherds, farmers, fishermen, artists. Renewing types of technology, alternative solutions to society's problems.

Lesser Known Food Group, Box 599, Lynwood California 90262. Contact Paul W. Jackson. Official title is International Association for Education, Development and Distribution of Lesser Known Food Plants and Trees. Aims to promote permanent agriculture and horticulture throughout the world. Publishes *Good and Wild*.

Worldwatch Institute, 1776 Massachusetts Ave. N.W., Washington, D.C. 20036. Phone 202 452-1999. Concentrates on emerging global problems and social trends. Publishes research in various booklets.

New Games Foundation, P. O. Box 7901, San Francisco, California 94120. Promotes and conceives new games based on crowd participation and noncompetition. Sponsors new games tournaments nationwide.

DUMP HEAP, P. O. Box 236, Lagunitas, California 94938. Unique group working to establish an experimental garden and seed/information exchange. Concerned with whole biological systems, from the perspective of people and plants. Publishes a journal and has seasonal seminars on weeds, tree crops, land trusts, plant breeding.

Recycled wood latticed into bean supports in San Francisco.

Seeds and Supplies

COMMUNITY GARDENERS WILL GET BETTER service and lower prices if they make bulk mail order purchases from seed and supply sources in their region. Send for catalogs of nearby seed houses. Determine your group's demand for various varieties of vegetables, flowers, herbs, trees, and other plants. Order all at once before the winter holidays slow the process down. If seeds are late, everyone's seeds are late. No gardener, however, should be restricted to only one source of seeds and supplies.

The Northeast

Johnny's Selected Seeds, Albion, Maine 04910. Emphasis on open pollinating varieties and saving your own seeds. Research on locally sufficient agriculture and tools. Ask about "seed swap."

Putney Nursery, U.S. Route 5, Putney, Vermont 05346. Ferns, wildflowers, culinary and aromatic herbs, perennials.

Joseph Harris Co., Moreton Farm, Rochester, New York 14624. Wide variety of vegetables and flowers.

Kelly Bros. Nurseries, Dansville, New York 14437. Vegetables, fruit and nut trees, berries, flowers, evergreens.

J. E. Miller Nurseries, 5060 West Lake Road, Canandaigua, New York 14424. Mostly berries, fruit trees, grapes, some vegetables.

Sterns Nurseries, Avenue E and Lehigh, Geneva, New York 14456. Berries, annuals, nut trees, some vegetables.

Stokes Seeds, Box 548, Buffalo, New York 14240. Wide variety of standard vegetables and flowers.

Lakeland Nurseries, Hanover, Pennsylvania 17331. Fruits, flowers, house plants, berries, nuts, vegetables. Lots of tropical and novelty plants.

The Natural Development Co., Bainbridge, Pennsylvania 17502. Organic vegetables, herbs, annuals, garden tools and accessories, organic food products, vitamins.

P. L. Rohrer & Bro., Inc., Lancaster County, Smoketown, Pennsylvania 17576. Vegetables, melons, flowers. Big on insecticides.

The South

George W. Park Seeds, P. O. Box 31, Greenwood, South Carolina 29647. Mostly flowers but pretty good selection of vegetables. Also accessories.

Wayside Gardens, Hodges, South Carolina 29695. Large selection of all varieties of flowers and shrubs. Some fruit trees, berries, grapes, nut trees. Catalog one dollar.

Otis S. Twilley Seed, P. O. Box 1817, Salisbury, Maryland 21801. Large selection of vegetables and flowers.

Tennessee Nursery & Seed, Tennessee Nursery Road, Cleveland, Tennessee 37311. Large selections of fruits, grapes, berries, nuts, vegetables, and melons. Also shrubs, shade and evergreen trees, garden accessories, annuals.

Stark Bros. Nurseries, Louisiana, Missouri 63353. Mostly fruit trees, berries, grapes. Some common vegetables and nut trees.

Whealy's True Seeds, RFD 2 KK, Princeton, Missouri 64673. Looking for old and unique varieties of food plants. Willing to swap seeds.

ER-OOGBA National Seed Order, c/o Stuart Leiderman, Drury, Missouri 65638. Bulk seed orders mostly of open pollinating varieties. Operates in winter only. Write in fall for listing of seeds. Working to provide "seed money" for Ozark Community Congress.

The Midwest

R. H. Shumway Seedsman, 628 Cedar St., Rockford, Illinois 61101. All types of vegetables, bulbs, flowers, some fruits. Great catalog with old-time woodcuts.

Burgess Seed & Plants, Galesburg, Michigan 49053. Vegetables, herbs, seeds for sprouting, grapes, berries, fruit trees, nut trees.

Dean Foster Nurseries, Hartford, Michigan 49057. Main emphasis on strawberries. Also other berries, fruit trees, vegetables, flowers, evergreens.

Farmer Seed & Nursery, Faribault, Minnesota 55021. All types of vegetables, fruit trees, flowers.

Ferndale Gardens, 709 Nursery Lane, Faribault, Minnesota 55021. Unusual fruits, vegetables, flowers, and house plants. Also standard flowers, trees, shrubs, fruits, worms and praying mantises.

L.L. Olds Seed, P. O. Box 1069, Madison, Wisconsin 53701. Wide variety of vegetables, herbs, berries, flowers, fruit trees. Also books, tools, accessories.

De Giorgi Company, 1411 Third Street, Council Bluffs, Iowa 51501. All varieties of vegetables, herbs, flowers, and planting information. Catalog thirty-five cents.

Henry Field Seed & Nursery, Shenandoah, Iowa 51602. Large variety of vegetables, berries, grapes, nut trees, fruits. Also novelty fruits and vegetables; trees, grasses, garden products, shrubs, annuals.

Earl May Seed & Nursery, Shenandoah, Iowa 51603. Annuals, house plants, trees, shrubs, bulbs, nut trees, vegetables, berries, fruit trees, garden products and accessories.

Inter-state Nurseries, Hamburg, Iowa 51644. Mostly flowers. Also fruit trees, berries, vegetables.

Farnam Companies, P. O. Box 12068, Omaha, Nebraska 68112. Mostly equipment: sprayers, tillers, log splitter, traps, fences, compost bins. Also fruit trees, berries, nuts.

Gurney Seed & Nursery, 2642 Page St., Yankton, South Dakota 57078. Novelty plants, bulbs, flowers, fruit trees, berries, house plants and gadgets.

The West

Redwood City Seed Company, P. O. Box 361, Redwood City, California 94964. Useful plants. Large selection of herbs, vegetables, fruits, nuts, berries, dye plants, and many other "usefuls." Wholesale bulk price list available free, on request.

D.V. Burrell Seed Growers, Rocky Ford, Colorado 81067. All varieties of vegetables and flowers. May request untreated seeds. Will separately package large orders for groups.

Armstrong Nurseries, P. O. Box 4060, Ontario, California 91761. Mostly roses. Some fruits, fruit trees, nut trees.

W. Atlee Burpee, 6350 Rutland Ave., Riverside, California 92505. Everything! One of the oldest and most respected seed houses.

Hudson World Seed Service, P. O. Box 1058, Redwood City, California 94064. Good source for many lesser known plants.

Kitazawa Seeds, 356 W. Taylor St., San Jose, California 95110. Uncommon vegetable varieties from China and Japan.

Spangler's Exotica Seeds, 820 S. Lorraine Blvd., Los Angeles, California 90005. Great source for all kinds of worldwide exotic seeds.

California Green Lacewings, 2521 Webb Ave., Alameda, California 94501. Green lacewings for biological control.

Rincon Vitova Insectories, P. O. Box 95, Oak View, California 93022. Predatory species of insects for biological pest management.

Nichols Garden Nursery, 1190 North Pacific Highway, Albany, Oregon 97321. Herbs, rare seeds, gourmet and novelty vegetables, teas, books, accessories.

Western Biological Control Labs, P. O. Box 1045, Tacoma, Washington 98401. Sources of natural pest predators.

Raised beds of kale and chard in Santa Cruz, California.

Facts and Fancies

CURRENT AND RELIABLE INFORMATION about gardening and communities is necessary for the continued growth of any community garden. In order to separate facts from fancy talk, gardeners must always search for and appraise new sources of information: books, booklets, publications, people. Of course, no information is more convincing than personal experience.

Each person has a responsibility to see that the information they gather and pass on to the group is accurate. This will reduce the flow of misinformation and encourage lively and precise communication.

Publications

Spotlight on Community Gardening. Official newsletter of Gardens for All. Write National Association for Gardening. Shelburne, Vermont 05482. Nationwide news. Monthly, $14 a year.

Self-Reliance, 1717 18th Street N.W., Washington, D.C. 20009. Bimonthly journal of Institute for Local Self-Reliance. Much emphasis on urban agriculture, energy and waste uses. Rate is $6 annually.

Organic Gardening and Farming Magazine, Rodale Press, 33 E. Minor St., Emmaus, Pennsylvania 18049. Monthly magazine always full of vital issues on gardening and farming in modern times. Subscription $7.85 yearly.

Rain, 2270 N.W. Irving, Portland, Oregon 97210. Monthly journal of appropriate technologies, including agriculture and horticulture. Rate is $10 yearly.

Tilth, Rt. 2, Box 190-A, Arlington, Washington 98223. Newsletter for farmers, community gardeners, and others who work the soil. Subscription $5 annually.

Over the Garden Fence, 3960 Cobblestone Dr., Dallas, Texas 75229. Magazine of gardening, herbs, child development, nutrition, self-sufficient homesteading, experimental gardens. Rate is $10 a year.

Acres, USA, 10227 E. 61st St., Raytown, Missouri 64133. Monthly magazine of ecologically-sound farming, gardening, and living.

Food Monitor, P. O. Box 1975, Garden City, New York 11530. Monthly newsletter of "analysis and action on food, land, and hunger." Yearly rate is $15.

Growup, edited by Susan O'Neill and John Forbes, The Greenhouse, 375 Laguna Honda Blvd., San Francisco, California 94131. Bay Area newsletter for community gardens.

Management Information Service Report, International City Management Assn., 1140 Connecticut Ave. N.W., Washington, D.C. 20036. April 1977, special issue on community gardens.

CoEvolution Quarterly, Box 428, Sausalito, California 94965. Thoughtful stories, resources, and facts about land use, communities, whole systems, and learning. Subscription $12 annually.

Mother Earth News, P. O. Box 70, Hendersonville, South Carolina 28739. Covers all aspects of self-reliant living. Subscription $10.

Good and Wild, Box 299, Lynwood, California 90262. Quarterly. Official but homey voice of a group concerned with introducing lesser known food plants. Subscription is $17.50 a year, including membership.

Booklets

Agriculture in the City, 1976. From Community Environmental Council, 109 E. De La Guerra, Santa Barbara, California 93101. Excellent intensive urban farm guide. Articles by members of this important active group about bees, chickens, city compost, conducting classes, and experiments with solar and methane energy.

Recreational Community Gardening by Susan York Drake, Bureau of Outdoor Recreation, Interior Dept., 1976. From U.S. Government Printing Office, Washington, D.C. 20402. The official handbook for recreational community garden programs. Organizing, insurance, potential problems, budget, funding sources, education, checklists.

Community Garden Handbook, 1976. From Hunger Action Center, Evergreen State College, Olympia, Washington 98505. Discusses community gardens based on case study of Seattle P-Patch Program. Includes contact list of other projects in the state.

Community Gardens Handbook by Susan J. Zurcher, 1977. From City Beautiful Council, 101 West Third St., Dayton, Ohio 45401. Planning and development techniques that created large one thousand family community garden project in Dayton.

Community Garden Procedural Manual, 1974. From Gardens for All, Inc., Box 371, Shelburne, Vermont 05482. Step-by-step rulebook for organizers from the old granddad of community garden groups. This book is too stodgy for many, but just right for others. Cost is ten dollars.

Community Gardening, 1976. From Los Angeles County, Dept. of Parks and Recreation, 155 W. Washington Blvd., Los Angeles, California 90015. Rule book for those who want to start or join a community garden in Los Angeles County.

Community Gardens in California by Rosemary Menninger, 1977. From Office of Planning and Research, 1400 10th St., Sacramento, California 95814. Very useful resource for Californians and others initiating and implementing community gardens. Includes recommendations for improvement.

Organizing Neighborhood Gardens for Your Community by New Hampshire Cooperative Extension, University of New Hampshire, Durham, New Hampshire 03824. Informative outline for those initiating projects in New England. Includes examples. Witty cover depicts spirit of many cultures gardening together. Free.

How to Manipulate the Media by Paul Kleyman, 1975. From San Francisco Art Commission, 165 Grove St., San Francisco, California 94102. Concise outreach handbook for community groups and nonprofit organizations working in large cities.

Conservation Tactics edited by Emily Jane Stover, U.S. Dept. of the Interior, 1976. From Superintendent of Documents, U.S. Printing Office, Washington, D.C. 20402. Useful presentation of land preservation techniques. Includes several case studies.

Cooperative Community Development, A Blueprint for Our Future edited by Joe Falk, 1975. From The Future Associates, P. O. Box 912, Shawnee Mission, Kansas 66201. "How to organize a cooperative neighborhood, block by block. Real estate acquisition, rehabilitation, new construction; cooperative purchasing and rental of all kinds of goods and services..." $2.95.

Weeds and What They Tell by E.E. Pfeiffer, 1970. From Bio-Dynamic Farming & Gardening Association, 17240 Los Alamos St., Granada Hills, California 91344. How weeds indicate the conditions of soils. Very useful. $1.80.

Handbook on Biological Control of Plant Pests. From Brooklyn Botanic Garden, Brooklyn, New York 11225. Good, practical introduction to pest management without chemicals. Just one of many booklets in a series of the best garden pamphlets in print.

The Community Land Trust — A Guide to a New Model for Land Tenure in America, 1972. From International Independence Institute, Center for Community Economic Development, 639 Massachusetts Ave., Suite 316, Cambridge, Massachusetts 02139.

Manual for holding and using land as a basis for community and economic development. Legal and organizational essentials.

Guidebook for Establishing Park-Open Space Foundations in California, 1977. Bureau of Outdoor Recreation, Pacific Southwest Region. Box 36062, 450 Golden Gate, San Francisco, California 94102. Inquire.

A Winter Harvest: A Handbook for Establishing Community Canning and Dehydration Centers by Lucy Gorham, 1976. From Maine Audubon Society, 53 Baxter Blvd., Portland, Maine 04101. Booklet costs twenty-five cents.

Community Canning Centers by Stephen Klein, 1977. From Center for Community Economic Development, 639 Massachusetts Ave., Cambridge, Massachusetts 02139. Overview of small-scale community canneries. He wonders why none of the centers he surveyed was self-sufficient. Two dollars.

The Institute for Local Self-Reliance (1717 18th Street N.W., Washington, D.C. 20009) has been working on neighborhood self-reliance in four areas: energy conservation, waste recycling, neighborhood development, and urban food production.

The institute publishes some of the best literature on these subjects. Send for a complete publications list. Here are their most significant publications to date.

Energy, Agriculture and Neighborhood Food Systems, seventy-five cents. Many examples of how urban agriculture can work.

Poisoned Cities and Urban Gardens, twenty-five cents. Discussion of air pollution and city-grown food.

Perspectives on Urban Agriculture, fifteen cents. Overview discussion of some current issues facing the growth of urban food production efforts.

Composting in the City, seventy-five cents. How to compost in urban areas on a neighborhood, municipal, and household scale. Sketches.

Urban Gardening Chart, three dollars. Two-color wall chart of planting information, nutrition, companion plants, pictures of harmful and beneficial insects.

How to Reach Your Local Bank (or Savings and Loan Institution), two dollars. A primer for investigating housing and economic conditions.

Books

The Unsettling of America by Wendell Berry, Sierra Club Books, 1977. Definitive thesis on what is wrong and right about agriculture and culture in America. Required reading.

Plants, Man and Life by Edgar Anderson, University of California Press, 1952. Fascinating accounts of the coevolution of plants and people. Traces the probable origins of agriculture back to village dump heaps.

Eating in Eden by Ruth Adams, Rodale Press, 1976. Worldwide look at the nutritional aspects of primitive diets.

Garden Cities of Tomorrow by Ebenezer Howard, M.I.T. Press, 1965. Reprint of 1898 open-space treatise by pioneer urban planner.

The Magic of Findhorn by Paul Hawken, Harper & Row, 1975. Tour of phenomenal northern Scotland community centered around its gardens.

The Secret Life of Plants by Peter Tompkins and Christopher Bird, Harper & Row, 1973. Accounts of extraordinary forces connecting plants and people. Includes writings on plants that read minds, open doors, and criticize music.

Food First by Frances Moore Lappe and Joseph Collins, Houghton Mifflin Co., 1977. Awesome document of worldwide agribusiness affronts to all human nature. Raises important land-use questions and exposes the myths of world hunger.

Diet for a Small Planet by Frances Moore Lappe, Ballantine Books, 1971. Account of the environmentally bankrupt and wasteful practices of growing and eating protein in the modern world. Full of good tasting recipes using complementary proteins. A classic modern cookbook.

The Lazy Man's Guide to Enlightenment by Thaddeus Golas, Seed Center, 1971. Brief, western-style handbook of eastern philosophy.

The Seven Laws of Money by Michael Phillips, Wordwheel/Random House, 1974. Best advice for obtaining foundation grants and other forms of funding. Includes the First Law: If you are doing the right thing, don't worry about money.

The Grass Roots Primer by James Robertson and John Lewallen, Sierra Club Books, 1975. Documents community resistance to environmental exploitation in the U.S. and Canada. "Steps to Power," useful appendix for community organizing and action.

The People's Land edited by Peter Barnes, Rodale Press, 1975. Articles about U.S. land-holding patterns. Discusses coops, changes in farm laws, community land trusts.

Radical Agriculture edited by Richard Merrill, Harper & Row, 1975. Hopeful essays for a changing agriculture. Includes land reform, urban agriculture, seed quality.

Forest Farming by J. Sholto Douglas and Robert A. de J. Hart, Watkins London, 1976. Advocates trees as the starting point for the design of gardens and farms. Includes trees categorized by function: fruits, nuts, oil, fodder, legumes.

Field Guide to Edible Wild Plants by Bradford Angier, Stackpole Books, 1974. All-color illustrated directory of wild foods. One of the best.

Stalking the Wild Asparagus by Euell Gibbons, McKay, 1962. Landmark handbook of edible wild foods by a great American naturalist.

Weeds, Guardians of the Soil by Joseph A. Cocannouer, Devin-Adair Co., 1950. How weeds protect soil, detoxify pollutants, break up hardpan, and coax water and minerals from deep hiding places.

Common Weeds of the United States by U.S.D.A., Dover Publications, 1971. Illustrated directory of major weeds. Map of each plant's distribution.

Everybody's A Winner by Tom Schneider, Little, Brown, & Co., 1976. Best book on new games and sports for everybody.

My Garden Companion by Jamie Jobb, Sierra Club/Scribners, 1977. Handy compendium of traditional garden techniques for children and other beginners. Big appendix. Lists several uncommon garden plants.

The City People's Book of Raising Food by Helga and William Olkowski, Rodale Press, 1975. How to begin urban gardens despite space and soil limitations. Discusses community gardens. A popular book.

Vegetables and Herbs: An Encyclopedia by Victor A. Tiedjens, Barnes & Noble Books, 1975. Very useful guide to most every vegetable and herb.

Planetary Planting by Louise Riotte, Simon & Schuster, 1975. Describes the effects of moon, planets, and stars on the growth and health of gardens.

Secrets of Companion Planting for Successful Gardening by Louise Riotte, Garden Way, 1975. Thorough listing of old-time planting lore, based on each plant's "likes" and "dislikes."

The Dictionary of Useful Plants by Nelson Coon, Rodale Press, 1974. Good resource organized according to plant families. All plants listed by scientific name. Also includes a section on how Indians used plants.

Underexploited Tropical Plants with Promising Economic Value by National Academy of Sciences, 1975. Important report on uncommon plants that can broaden the diversity of world agriculture. New plants useful for food, oils, forage, soil improving.

Stocking Up by the editors, Rodale Press, 1973. Best all-round handbook on canning, freezing, drying, and other ways to preserve food.

Complete Guide to Home Canning, Preserving and Freezing by U.S.D.A., Dover, 1973. Seven manuals reprinted in a single volume.

Additional Reading

The World in Your Garden by Wendell H. Camp et al., National Geographic, 1957.

Plants and Man: The Story of Our Basic Food by H.L. Edlin, Aldus Books Ltd., 1967.

The First Farmers: The Emergence of Man by Jonathan Norton Leonard, Time-Life Books, 1973.

The Geography of Life by Wilfred T. Neill, Columbia Press, 1969.

A Treasury of American Indian Herbs by Virginia Scully, Crown, 1970.

A Manual of Plant Names by C. Chicheley Plowden, George Allen & Unwin Ltd., 1968.

A Gardener's Guide to Better Soil by Gene Logsdon, Rodale Press, 1975.

The Food-and-Heat-Producing Solar Greenhouse by Bill Yanda and Rick Fisher, John Muir Publications, 1976.

The Complete Book of Fruits and Vegetables by Francesco Bianchini and Francesco Corbetta, Crown, 1975.

How to Grow More Vegetables Than You Ever Thought Possible on Less Land Than You Can Imagine by John Jeavons, Ecology Action Center, 1974.

How to Grow Vegetables and Fruits by the Organic Method by J.I. Rodale, Rodale Press, 1973.

The Basic Book of Organic Gardening by Robert Rodale, Editor, Ballantine Books, 1971.

Crockett's Victory Garden by James Crockett, Little, Brown & Co., 1977.

Eat Well on a Dollar a Day by Bill and Ruth Kaysing, Chronicle Books, 1975.

The Organic Gardener by Catharine Osgood Foster, Vintage, 1972.

The New York Times Book of Vegetable Gardening by Joan Lee Faust, A & W Visual Library, 1975.

Moon Sign Book and Daily Planetary Guide by Llewellyn Publications, annually.

The Common Insects of North America by Lester A. Swan and Charles S. Papp, Harper & Row, 1972.

Beneficial Insects by L. Swan, Harper & Row, 1964.

The Complete Handbook of Plant Propagation by R.C.M. Wright, Macmillan, 1973.

How to Grow Your Weeds by Audrey Wynn Hatfield, Collier Books, 1974.

Plants as Therapy by Eldon McDonald, Popular Library, 1977.

The People's Almanac by David Wallechninsky and Irving Wallace, Doubleday, 1975.

Films

Biological Control, Cooperative Extension, University of California, Berkeley, California 94720. Film for rent or purchase. Theory and practice of biological control of insect pests. Close-ups of familiar pests, beneficial predators, and parasites. Thirty minutes.

Film Library, Brooklyn Botanic Garden, 1000 Washington Ave., Brooklyn, N.Y. 11225. Excellent films for rent or purchase including *Planting and Transplanting*. Write for catalog.

MacMillan Horticultural Films, 24 MacQuestan Parkway So., Mt. Vernon, N.Y. 10550. Several good films including those produced by Brooklyn Botanic.

Magus Films, 2 Embarcadero Center, Suite 2780, San Francisco, California 94111. Produces environmental films. *Down to Earth Living* is about Integral Urban House.

Modern Talking Picture Service, 2323 New Hyde Park Road, New Hyde Park, N.Y. 11040. Ortho films as well as many others. Films are free, so is catalog.

Ortho Garden Films, 200 Bush St., San Francisco, California 94104. No charge to schools, garden clubs, and horticultural groups. The commercial chemical pitch varies in intensity, but the cultural information tends to be accurate.

Index

donations, 47, 55, 56, 64, 82
double digging, 120-21
Drake, Susan, 58-59
Dr. Grow, 53, 54
ducks, 37, 39
DUMP HEAP, 156-57
dumps, 20, 56, 115

E

earthworms, 114, 115, 119
easement, affirmative, 82
ecology, 129
EFNEP (Expanded Food and Nutrition Education Program), 62, 99
eggplant, 109, 132
elephant manure, 117
employee gardens, 38, 73, 85
enclosure acts, 72
Environmental Response, 79
Europe, 68, 72-73
experimental gardens, 96

F

fallow fields, 71
families, of people, 34-35, 41, 94, 129; of plants, 22, 69, 106-13, 129
farmland, 17, 38, 62, 71, 82, 152
farm machines, 17-18, 35, 71; workers, 17
fees, 21, 59-60, 96
fence material, 56
fences, 71-72, 87-89, 140, 141
Fenway Garden, 30, 74, 90, 139-40
fertility, 122
fertilizer, 115
finances, *see* money
fish, 21, 37
Flowers, James, 140
flyers, 49, 50, 116
fluids in plants, 123
followers, 45
food, 16-18, 20, 21, 34, 37, 38, 71-72, 77, 90, 92, 110, 116, 117, 139, 144, 155; preparation, 20, 34; prices, 17, 18, 144; quality, 21; storage, 17, 34, 74, 144
forests, 114, 115
formal community gardens, 21
Fort Mason Garden, 59
4-H Clubs, 58, 61, 70
foxglove, 108
Friend, Gil, 79, 116, 151-156
frost, 122
fruit, 96, 108, 113, 118
future building sites, 76

G

garden, colonies, 72; forms, 35, 38; laying out of, 44-45, 90-92; life forms, 106, 129; materials, 56; neglected, 97; plots, 77, 87, 90-92
gardening, motivations, 39; precedents, 71
garden person, 47, 75, 77, 89, 97, 98, 116, 122, 123, 131, 132
Girl Scouts, 61, 70
goats, 37, 39
goldenrod, 76
goosefoot family (*Chenopodiaceae*), 109
gophers, 138
gourd family (*Cucurbitaceae*), 108, 131
gourds, 96, 108
government, 21, 60, 81-82; federal, 57, 62-65; local, 60-61, 65, 81-82; people in, 60; state, 61-62, 65; surplus land belonging to, 75, 81-82
greenhouse, 23, 78, 150, 152-53
ground cherry, 29, 98, 109
grow and share plots, 95-96
Guatemala, 17
guerilla gardens, 156-57

H

Hamilton, Calvin, 73
hand cultivation, 119
handicapped, access for, 90
Harrisburg, Pennsylvania, 27, 31, 158
harrow, disc, 17, 118
Hartford, Connecticut, 98
harvest, 131
Hayes, Robert, 54, 63-64
health, 21, 36-37, 38-39, 102-05, 129, 130, 135, 139
heavy metals, *see also* soil, heavy metals in, 79, 117
Henley family, 31
herbicides, 92-93, 98, 102
HEW (Health, Education and Welfare), 61, 62
highway sites, 76, 78, 86
hives, bee, 137
Honolulu, Hawaii, 63
hoses, 78, 122, 123
hospital land, 82
Houston, Texas, 62
HUD (Housing and Urban Development), 57, 63
humus, 114-16, 117, 119, 122
hunger, 34, 38
hydroponics, 153-54

I

incorporation, 56, 59
Indianapolis, Indiana, 29, 59-60, 144, 159
Indonesia, 73
informal community gardens, 21
insects, 47, 129, 134-39
Institute for Local Self-Reliance, 79, 116, 151-54, 155-56
insurance, 56, 58-59, 94, 96
Integral Urban House, 78, 117-18
integrated pest management, 136-39
intensive plantings, 119-21
interplanting, 121, 134-35, 136
investment properties, 76
irrigation system, 123

J

Japan, 38, 73
Jomo, 22

K

Kansas City stockyard, 18
Keys, Gladys, 144, 147
kids in gardens, 90, 94
Kingman, Frances, 30, 139-40
Knepley, Clayton, 26
Kourik, Robert, 156-57

L

Labor, Department of, 63
lamb's quarters, 76, 98, 110
land, 38, 43, 56, 61, 64, 68-72, 75-77, 81, 83, 150; common, 38, 71-72; donations, 82; government, 61, 75, 81-82; owners of, 58-59, 81-83; trust, 23, 83, 150; use, 62, 71-72
leadership, *see also* seed bunch, 44-47
lead in soil, 77, 78-79
leaf mold, 115, 116
lease, 82, 83
legume family (*Leguminosae*), 108, 111
leisure gardens, 20
lesser known food plants, 26, 38, 96
lettuce, wild, 98
liberty gardens, 20, 73
life forms, *see* garden, life forms